The Energy Intelligent Business

The Energy Intelligent Business

The Science and Soul of Sustainable Success

Shelley Poovey

Published by Game Changer Publishing

Paperback ISBN: 979-8-90158-302-9

Hardcover ISBN: 979-8-90158-151-3

Digital ISBN: 979-8-90158-152-0

www.GameChangerPublishing.com

To the clients and colleagues who trusted me enough to explore this work alongside me: your questions, challenges, insights, and willingness to engage with the process helped shape it into what it has become today.

To those who saw something in my work before I fully trusted it myself and who encouraged me to create something of my own rather than repeat what already existed: your belief helped me recognize that what I was discovering was not a single method but a synthesis of many disciplines, experiences, and ways of seeing the world.

And to the teachers, both direct and indirect, whose wisdom made this work possible; this book does not exist in isolation. It is part of a larger body of knowledge created by countless people seeking to understand how we grow, heal, and create new possibilities.

May this work contribute, in its own way, to expanding what we believe is possible for ourselves and for the world we share.

Advance Praise

"If you're tired of the constant 'hustle' and looking for a business strategy that actually feels sustainable, The Energy Intelligent Business is a total breath of fresh air. Shelley Poovey shares her own raw personal journey to show how neuroscience and spirituality can work together, proving that success doesn't have to come at the cost of your well-being. It's a practical, heart-centered guide that helps you tune into your 'thinking body' and lead with a deep sense of alignment and ease."

— **David Trotter,** *Publisher of Awakened Magazine,*

"The Energy Intelligent Business gives conscious entrepreneurs a doorway they can walk through to not only help themselves and their work, but to help their clients as well. Shelley speaks to moments we've all experienced, but might not have been able to put words to. It's an enticing read for someone who wants to tap more into the innate wisdom the body has always held. Shelley is an excellent guide for this. She's walked the path, dealt with the ups and downs.

This book can help you 'follow your yes' the same way Shelley followed her yes in college."

— **Richard Taliaferro,** *Career Transition Coach*

Read This First

Just to say thank you for buying and reading this book, I have some free bonus gifts waiting for you, plus an open invitation to book a free call with me directly!

Scan the QR code below to claim your gifts and schedule your complimentary session today, no strings attached!

Scan the QR Code Here:

The Energy Intelligent Business

The Science and Soul of Sustainable Success

Shelley Poovey

Contents

Foreword

To the reader who has chosen to turn this book in your hands—thank you for being here and for daring to look beyond the familiar. Lean into the unknown and you will be richly rewarded.

At some point in many careers, a quiet shift begins. The numbers on the board look strong, the calendar is full, and the business is growing. Yet beneath it all a subtle disquiet stirs—a feeling that something essential is missing, a disconnect you can't quite name. I have seen this pattern play out again and again—in boardrooms, in leadership teams, in conversations with high-performing founders and executives I advise. I have lived through my own stirring and responded to the voice of intuition. We are taught to optimize, scale, and compete; we're trained to focus on metrics, outcomes, and performance. We learn how to manage results but not the energy, beliefs, and patterns that drive them. And the most juice is squeezed from harkening the voice within and diving deeply into soul work.

That is why *The Energy Intelligent Business* is such a timely and important contribution. Shelley Poovey offers a different lens—one that sees business not merely as a set of strategies or transactions but as an intelligent, responsive ecosystem. One that reflects not only what we do, but also how we think, lead, and show up.

In this work, intuition is not abstract or elusive. It's practical and trainable and, when developed, becomes a powerful advantage—helping leaders navigate complexity with clarity rather than control. What I find especially compelling is how grounded this approach is. Shelley integrates neuroscience, psychology, and embodied awareness in a way that feels both accessible and actionable. She shows that the beliefs we carry—shaped by our experiences, environments, and conditioning—don't simply influence how we think. They shape how we lead, how we make decisions, how we handle pressure, and ultimately the results we create.

The heart of the book is the BizAttune framework—a vortex that aligns mind, body, and business into a single coherent system. By treating the business as its own energetic field, Shelley demonstrates how clarity and performance can reinforce one another rather than compete. This vortex is not a mystical idea; it's an actionable model that translates intuitive insight into measurable outcomes, helping you untangle limiting beliefs, restore vitality, and align action with purpose.

Through real stories and client experiences, she shows that performance begins with perception. When you pull back the lens and shift the way you see your work, you change how you engage with it—and that's where meaningful, lasting change begins.

This is not another book about pushing harder or doing more. Nor is it a formulaic recipe that you mimic like thousands of others. Instead, it reframes growth as an inside-out process. Concepts such as alchemy and manifestation are brought down to earth, made practical—tools for identifying and releasing limiting beliefs, restoring energy, and aligning action with purpose in a measurable way.

The result is a different kind of business—one that operates less like a machine and more like a dynamic system that evolves with you. One where clarity, energy, and performance are not in tension but in alignment.

For entrepreneurs, executives, and purpose-driven leaders ready to move beyond burnout-driven success into something more sustainable and meaningful, this book is an invitation. It's a reminder that you don't have to choose between momentum and meaning—you can build both, intentionally. Welcome to your soul journey.

If you're ready for this shift, you are holding the right book. I look forward to seeing how this work shapes your journey.

Dr. Gina Lepore

Founder, MACH4 Ventures

Investor, Advisor & Executive Coach

Introduction

In my many years of leading Peak Performance Coaching, I discovered something surprising: for many people, the mere thought of reaching peak performance brings on feelings of dread and even anxiety. On the surface, they like the idea of the success they want to create. They want the impact, the income, the freedom, the recognition. Yet many cannot imagine waking up every day as that version of themselves—sustaining that level of visibility, responsibility, and output without losing themselves in the process.

This book is about why that happens, and how a different approach to performance allows success to become sustainable, intuitive, and aligned rather than depleting.

We live in a culture that quietly reinforces the idea that success requires self-sacrifice. Many of the high-performing professionals I work with share this pattern. They give endlessly to their work yet feel a quiet dissonance inside. I was no exception. For me, this manifested as sacrificing my personal life and health in pursuit of the impact I felt called to create through my work in health and healing. There were moments where I could feel something wasn't working, even when everything looked like it should have been. I didn't have language for it yet, but I could feel the cost.

Throughout this journey, I realized that while I had the right intentions and passions, I was going about it in the wrong way. My business began to reflect this back to me. My business became my teacher, a mirror that showed me exactly where I was out of alignment and what I needed to heal. This shift, from forcing outcomes to learning from the system itself, became the foundation for everything that followed.

The roots of our cultural fixation on productivity did not emerge by accident. One of the most influential forces behind this orientation is what has come to be known as the

Protestant work ethic—a framework that links hard work, discipline, and frugality to moral virtue. This ethic shaped how to interpret worth and success.

At its core was the idea that work itself was a calling. Labor wasn't simply a way to survive; it was believed to reflect a person's inner character. Diligence was elevated to a moral duty, while rest and idleness were seen as threats. Self-denial and restraint became the expected norms, reinforcing a culture where accumulation and industriousness were seen as signs of responsibility and even divine favor.

Max Weber argued that this mindset didn't just influence individual behavior—it helped lay the psychological groundwork for modern capitalism.[1] Over generations, this mindset created a collective narrative equating productivity with virtue and financial success with proof of worthiness.

The legacy of this ethic is still visible today, woven into the subtle beliefs that reward constant doing over intentional being. Many of the patterns we observe in high achievers—such as working through illness, feeling guilty when resting, striving for perfection, or treating overwork as a badge of honor—echo these inherited messages.

Across industries, professionals are quietly questioning a model of success that demands relentless productivity while eroding health, relationships, and meaning.

Our productivity culture reflects this conditioning. We push through forty-plus-hour work weeks, drag ourselves from task to task, and collapse into the evenings with no energy left for movement or pleasure. We take cough suppressants and medications not to heal, but to keep going. We override signals, mute sensations, and silence the body's communication to remain productive. This way of living has been passed down through generations, and the wisdom of the body has stayed dormant as a result.

In much of Western culture, the body has long been treated as something secondary to the mind—less trustworthy, something to discipline or override. We're socialized to ignore its signals, silence its sensations, and value the mind's logic and productivity above everything else. Yet the body was never meant to be the lesser half. When we separate mind from body, we disconnect from our wholeness.

---

1. Weber, M. (1905). The Protestant Ethic and the Spirit of Capitalism.

There is an innate flow between these two aspects of ourselves. Our natural state is wholeness. It's the state in which the body is not something we analyze but something we inhabit—a state I call being a "thinking body," where cognition and sensation are not separate but part of a single, living intelligence.

Understanding this history helps us recognize that the compulsion to overwork is not just personal—it is cultural, ancestral, and deeply conditioned. Naming these inherited beliefs provides a pathway to question them, disentangle ourselves from them, and ultimately reclaim a more sustainable and compassionate relationship with our work, our bodies, and our purpose.

As I questioned these inherited patterns in my life, I noticed something subtle yet undeniable. When I stopped overriding my internal signals and started listening to my intuition, decisions felt different. They required less force. Unexpected connections began to form. Insights would arise before I had fully reasoned them out. I started following small intuitive nudges—what felt aligned rather than impressive—and those choices often unfolded into opportunities I could not have predicted.

My name is Shelley Poovey, and I am an International Coaching Federation (ICF) Professional Certified Coach with a master's degree in health and human performance. My journey has been about reconciling two worlds—the measurable and the mystical—to help others find harmony between purpose and performance. I've spent over twenty-five years in the health and wellness space, with the last 10 years dedicated to exploring the philosophy and science of alchemy and manifestation.

When I look back now, what strikes me most is how long I spent trying to make my business successful through willpower, discipline, and effort—echoes of the Protestant work ethic woven into my bones. In the early years of my career, I treated the business like an extension of myself, something to fix or force into shape. But the real acceleration happened when I finally allowed my business to separate from me and become a living laboratory that acted like an Olympic coach, guiding me to optimal performance. This aligned with many hidden or devalued gifts and talents that served an important purpose for myself and others, including healing the inheritance of overwork and scarcity that was keeping me from embodying success as a state of being to be nourished by rather than achieving.

My goal is to help individuals break through barriers in their personal and professional lives, particularly at the intersection of wellness and business. The wellness component is essential because the more I learned to trust intuition, the more I noticed that it organized outcomes in ways that strategy alone never had. Only later did I discover that what I was experiencing personally was something already being studied at the highest levels of business leadership.

Research has shown that many successful executives rely heavily on intuition when making high-stakes decisions. A Harvard Business Review study found that CEOs who consistently trusted their intuition achieved some of the strongest business growth.[2] Yet intuition is often discussed cautiously in executive circles. Leaders may acknowledge the role of data and analysis publicly, while privately recognizing that many of their most important decisions involve pattern recognition, experience, and a form of knowing that emerges before it can be fully explained.

While developing my method and conducting market research during graduate school, I interviewed senior executives and professionals about how they approached decision-making. What emerged was a striking gap between what leaders publicly attribute to analytical reasoning and what actually happens behind the scenes. Many rely on intuition far more than they openly acknowledge. In environments where uncertainty is high and information is incomplete, intuition becomes a crucial performance advantage.

In a world where artificial intelligence can process enormous volumes of information in seconds, the uniquely human advantage may lie not in computation but in perception—the capacity to integrate subtle signals, lived experience, and embodied awareness into clear judgment.

At the same time, the nature of work itself is undergoing profound transformation. Advances in artificial intelligence are rapidly reshaping knowledge work. Tasks once requiring specialized training—from drafting reports to analyzing data—can now be assisted or completed by machine-learning systems. Economic reports from organizations such as the World Economic Forum and McKinsey & Company estimate that a significant percentage of professional tasks will be augmented or automated within the coming

2. Huang, L. (2025). How CEOs hone and harness their intuition. Harvard Business Review.

decade. Major news outlets including *The New York Times*, *The Wall Street Journal*, and *The Economist* have documented how automation is beginning to transform professions that were once considered stable and secure.

For many professionals, this shift raises an important question: if information itself is no longer scarce, what will distinguish human judgment from machine output?

Many high performers are not struggling because they lack opportunity. They are struggling because the definition of success they inherited no longer feels meaningful.

Careers themselves are also evolving. Instead of climbing a single organizational ladder, many professionals now build portfolio lives—combining roles, projects, and ventures that change over time. In this environment, success depends less on rigid planning and more on the ability to adapt, experiment, and make clear decisions amid uncertainty. Leadership researchers increasingly describe this capacity as adaptability. Ilana Golan, founder of LEAP Academy, refers to it as the Adaptability Quotient (AQ)—the ability to continually evolve one's identity, skill set, and influence in response to rapidly changing environments.[3]

The biological foundations of intuition offer another layer of understanding. The parts of the brain involved in intuitive processing are closely related to systems that regulate homeostasis.[4] Homeostasis is the self-regulating process by which biological systems maintain stability while adjusting to changing conditions. It allows an organism to maintain internal balance even as the external environment shifts. In practical terms, this means our internal regulatory systems are constantly allocating resources to maintain equilibrium, especially when there is a significant gap between what our bodies need and what performance demands of us.

Life pushes us to run in sympathetic overdrive (fight/flight). Being in constant overdrive disrupts this processing, which happens on a different network (rest/digest). It's not just that we are ignoring intuition; it's that intuition processed in overwhelm is predictive, based on creating safety, and taking control through a fear response. Insights reflect this and are reactive. This can interfere with health and well-being and keep homeostasis

---

3. Ilana Golan, "Home," *Ilana Golan*,https://www.ilanagolan.com https://www.ilanagolan.com

4. Damasio, A. (2018). The strange order of things: Life, feeling, and the making of cultures. New York: Pantheon.

calibrated to overwhelm, dysregulation, inflammation, and all the symptoms that come with that (insomnia, digestive disruption, chronic stress, and stress-related illnesses).

The type of intuition we will discuss in this book—effective decision-making under uncertainty—cannot be accessed from that network.[5] By working to develop it, we can recalibrate homeostasis to rest/digest and help maintain homeostasis at that level—even in uncertain, high-pressure, or high-stress situations.

Unlike other peak performance models that push you to level up through force and discipline, this approach develops peak performance in a way that is deeply personal, sustainable, and aligned with who you are. It gives you a process that manifests outcomes that support you in becoming the version of yourself you envision, rather than demanding that you immediately perform as that version before you feel ready. Every challenge, setback, or obstacle becomes part of your personal success formula. Instead of derailing you, those moments engage you. They become opportunities to operate in flow, aligned with purpose and meaning, even in difficulty.

There's personal intuition, professional intuition, and a type of expert intuition we'll explore in depth in this book: business intuition. Business intuition draws on both your professional expertise and the specialized skills developed within your field. I have also found that many people unconsciously merge their personal energy system with their business. When this happens, the business begins to feel heavy, overwhelming, or unsustainable because identity and performance become fused together.

Columbia Business School teaches Quantitative Intuition™, which is similar to my concept of business intuition.[6] Both rely on a combination of data, experience, and gut instincts to address real-world challenges in the face of uncertainty. An example of using both quantitative and business intuition would be a nurse who knows which tests a patient needs or which action to take when every second counts.[7] This blend of knowledge and intuition is something that evolves in relation to the work that you do.

---

5. McEwen, B. S. (1998). Stress, adaptation, and disease: Allostasis and allostatic load. Annals of the New York Academy of Sciences, 840, 33–44.

6. Frank, C. J., Magnone, P. F., & Netzer, O. (2022). Decisions over decimals: Striking the balance between intuition and information. Wiley.

7. Klein, G. (1998). Sources of Power: How People Make Decisions.

In this book, I treat business as a distinct consciousness system, what I refer to as a "vortex," with its own filters, patterns, and potential. This vortex operates as a North Star: a guiding intelligence that organizes aligned circumstances, supports sustainable success, and leads you toward the fulfillment of your personal peak potential.

Over the years, I have referred to this work by many names as it evolved in real time. At different stages, I called it Business Alchemy, Biz Alchemy and Manifestation, the Business Vortex, Business Energetics, or simply "the work." Each name reflected a different facet of the same underlying methodology: transforming internal interference into aligned performance by working with both your personal energy system and your business as a distinct field of intelligence.

As the framework matured, I began referring to it under one integrated name: BizAttune. BizAttune represents the unified method you will encounter throughout this book. It weaves together all parts of the work into a single, coherent system. Rather than separate techniques, they are components of one process designed to recalibrate how you relate to performance, resources, decision-making, and sustainable success.

When you work with your business as a separate energy field while stabilizing your personal peak state, you release the pressure of carrying everything alone. Two aligned systems—yourself and your business—begin to operate cohesively. As clarity increases, interference patterns that once distorted decision-making begin to dissolve. When you thrive, your business thrives, and when your business becomes attuned, it begins to support you in return.

I also share with you the powerful process of unpacking alchemy and manifestation for business. Alchemy, as I define it here, is the process of transforming what blocks us into what empowers us. Manifestation is how that transformation becomes visible in the world—through action, energy, and aligned outcomes.

Many people approach manifestation as if it were a kind of "Mad Lib," assuming that if they insert the right action into the formula, they will automatically receive the desired result. In reality, manifestation rarely functions as a simple cause-and-effect equation. Each person has a unique manifesting blueprint. By studying how your system responds to opportunities, setbacks, and resources, you begin to understand how your personal peak performance unfolds.

As this approach evolved, I saw that periods of financial contraction or limited resources were not always signs of failure. Sometimes they emerged as part of a deeper recalibration process—an invitation to clarify motivation, reconnect with purpose, and examine how resources were being used. When these patterns are understood and integrated, the next phase of growth often unfolds on a far more stable foundation.

In the chapters that follow, we will explore how intuition emerges from the body's regulatory systems and how developing business intuition can reduce stress and overwhelm while supporting clear decision-making in uncertain environments.

The real peak performance advantage will belong to those who cultivate intuitive intelligence in ways that technology cannot replicate.

There isn't one definitive path to success that works for everyone, but you deserve to find yours. You deserve to feel energized in both your personal and professional life. Through this book, my intention is to help you move beyond simply thinking about that possibility and to begin living it.

Chapter One

The Thinking Body

Intuition first took root in my life long before I had the language for it. From choosing a college to following a spontaneous "yes," every decision I made in my younger years was laying the groundwork for how I would later understand business intuition and the science of manifestation.

I started college in the fall of 1992, right after graduating high school. I attended UNC-Chapel Hill on the advice of my French teacher. I remember one day in the hallway, she approached me and asked, "Have you thought about your future?"

I replied, "Not really. I think I'll just do what everyone else is doing and apply to local schools." I grew up in a small suburb of Charlotte, and the expectation was that I would go to a school close enough to commute from home. She encouraged me to consider UNC-Chapel Hill, suggesting that I think bigger. She knew no one was supporting me in this process, much less encouraging me to apply to the best public school in the state. UNC is a prestigious school with more opportunities than I would get locally. She saw my potential and encouraged it when no one else was. I was truly grateful.

When I started college in the fall of '92, I felt overwhelmed. I applied to UNC without visiting, so I didn't know much about it. I did not have a strong support network at school, but I was still involved in various arts programs back in my hometown, so I often commuted home on the weekends to participate in those activities. My best friend went to a different school and sent me a breakup letter with no explanation. I had some arguments and misunderstandings with another childhood friend, which caused that friendship to fade as well.

My first year at college was a difficult adjustment—away from home, unsupported, losing lifelong friends—with not a clue what I was doing. I didn't know it then, but those early disorienting months were training me to listen for a deeper signal. Even then, I was learning what it meant to find my own blueprint for success, not one handed to me by others.

After completing my first year, I took a summer job working in a restaurant. While doing repetitive tasks like food prep and cutting vegetables, I allowed my mind to wander, to consider what might be possible for my future. That idle, rhythmic focus was my first lived experience of pre-conscious integration—where the mind quietly organizes reality before awareness catches up. I would later study this brain mechanism in cognitive psychology, learning how such moments create insight and actionable inspiration. Research on the brain's default mode network shows that during periods of rest and mind-wandering, the brain reactivates and reorganizes information, supporting memory consolidation and the emergence of new insights.[1]

I took a year off from school to pursue my dream of dancing to decide what I wanted to study when I returned. I auditioned for several color guard groups, a form of pageantry that doesn't require formal dance training to perform at a high level. I was accepted into a group in Boston. I moved there for the year. It was a truly life-changing experience for me. I spent my days dancing and my evenings thinking about what was next. Movement and practicing for my show were repetitive activities that distracted me from overthinking. Just like the summer I spent chopping veggies in a restaurant kitchen, I used that same repetitive process to arrive at the conclusion that I'd like to study psychology.

A year later, I re-enrolled in UNC, this time as a sophomore and psychology major. I matured a lot during my gap year, learning to be on my own without my family's support. I had gained a lot of confidence and fulfilled a commitment to myself, accomplishing something I had always wanted to do. I enrolled in psychology courses with a renewed sense of discipline and clarity of purpose. This was very validating for me; I started making the dean's list each semester and building new friendships.

---

1. Joshi, D. et al. (2026). The default mode network: where spontaneous thought and memory consolidation meet. Current Opinion in Behavioral Sciences.

One day, a friend invited me to a dance audition for a dance company at UNC. She didn't want to go alone, so I joined her. I was one of 150 dancers. While I had experience in creative arts, I lacked formal dance training. Despite feeling out of place among so many formally trained dancers who knew ballet and jazz, I approached the audition thinking, *It's just a free dance class, no big deal.*

Two days later, when results were posted in the dance studio, I didn't even bother checking. There was no part of me that believed I would get in. To my surprise, I received a call from my friend who said, "Congratulations! You got into the dance company!" I was shocked, as only a handful of people were accepted. This opportunity opened a new door for me, allowing me to perform and continue my dance training alongside my studies. I eagerly accepted and began taking dance classes in addition to my psychology courses.

I enrolled in a course called cognitive psychology, which focuses on understanding how the mind works. During one of my professor's office hours, I asked a question about cognitive psychology within the broader field of cognitive science. This field explores the mind through various lenses, including psychology, neuroscience, medicine, artificial intelligence, computer science, and philosophy. Instead of answering my question directly, my professor asked me, "What do you think the answer is?"

I shared my thoughts with him. He paused before saying, "I think you have a really good grasp of this field. Do you want a job?"

As a sophomore, I accepted a research assistant position with that professor, working in psychophysics—the study of how physical stimuli are translated into perceptual experience. My initial work focused on auditory perception, examining how the brain processes sound. Our goal was to understand how the brain interacts with sensation to create perception.

This sparked my curiosity about how the mind works and how consciousness itself organizes reality—what I now call the "intersection of science and spirit." It planted the seed that something intangible like intuition could be observed, described, and even replicated.

As I continued working in the lab, my interest in cognitive psychology deepened. I attended lectures across campus and found myself navigating two distinct sides of my identity: one as an artist and the other as a scientist. I've always loved dancing and writing poetry—even winning writing contests as a child. At the same time, I was drawn to science, especially psychology, from a research perspective. I felt caught between these two identities. The performing arts were a true passion, but my family discouraged me from pursuing them, emphasizing practicality and responsibility—urging me to focus on something more stable, like science.

One day, a friend invited me to a colloquium hosted by a professor in the computer science department. She was speaking on visual perception, and I found the talk fascinating. It explored how the brain constructs visual experience and how that process informs our broader understanding of cognition. Afterward, I asked if I could meet with her to continue the conversation. During that meeting, she offered me a research assistant position, and I transitioned from auditory to visual perception research, remaining within psychophysics but now studying how the brain processes visual information. It felt like a stroke of luck, with doors opening at every turn.

On the advice of my cognitive psychology professor, who told me I would likely need a PhD in psychology, I learned that studying computer science would be beneficial. He suggested I pursue my undergraduate degree in computer science because programming would be a requirement in graduate school. So I switched my major from psychology to computer science and began taking relevant courses.

My principal investigator in the visual perception lab where I was working required me to enroll in a graduate-level course she was teaching. So there I was, a newly declared computer science major, stepping into a graduate seminar filled with engineering and computer science students. Honestly, I felt overwhelmed.

I distinctly remember the day I went to that first graduate class. I stepped into the elevator to head to the graduate-level classrooms when my introductory computer science professor followed me in. He asked where I was going, and I told him about the course involving concepts I hadn't formally studied yet. I was deeply intimidated.

He gave me some of the best advice I've ever received: "Good for you. You need to put yourself in rooms full of people who are smarter than you. That's how you'll learn and excel." I took that advice to heart.

At the height of all that, the principal investigator in the visual perception lab where I was working announced her retirement. She was 42 years old and at the top of her career. She was a well-known researcher in her field with numerous publications, textbook citations, and significant grant funding. In every sense of the academic world, she was very successful.

She stated she was retiring to spend more time with her family, which was partially true. However, she pulled me into her office and said, "I feel like I owe you a real explanation. If this is all I ever do, I will have missed out on what really matters in life."

She explained that the academic world is extremely competitive, with constant competition for grants. The research often serves purposes that don't benefit humanity, such as prioritizing the development of weapons for government contracts.

She was a mentor who took me under her wing—a remarkable woman, embodying everything I considered to be success. Yet, she told me, "This isn't it."

My mentor looked at me and said, "You're smart. You're capable. You can do anything you want to do. And you're young enough to go ahead and pursue it. The world needs your passion. It needs your joy." She encouraged me to pursue and invest in anything else I might want to do. Her words meant a lot to me because I had always been discouraged from following my passions.

In my family, practicality was the highest virtue. Stability, security, and self-sufficiency were prioritized over self-expression. There was also a subtle message that desire could cloud judgment, that wanting too much could lead to disappointment. Creative ambition was often met with caution, and there was an unspoken understanding that dreams were fragile, that virtue lies in hard work and humility, not personal ambition. Passion was something you felt quietly, perhaps privately—but you did not build your life around it. Over time, I internalized the idea that joy was secondary to duty.

So here was someone I looked up to, giving me full permission to chase my dreams. Though I didn't immediately take her advice, I decided to stay for another semester to explore my options.

One day, while walking on campus, I came across a captivating flyer. It depicted a woman curled in a fetal position, showcasing every subtle muscle in her back. Her clothes draped over her body beautifully; the imagery was simply sublime. The flyer announced a year-long training program in dance therapy and depth psychology. Even though the first meeting had already happened, I called the number on the flyer.

The woman who answered encouraged me, saying, "Absolutely! Join late. It's good." My whole body trembled with excitement and terror. I was breaking all the rules about being practical. At the same time, I questioned the value of something like this, wondering how it could ever be financially viable. In the end I threw caution to the wind.

This was the first time I experienced alchemy in action, transformation through truth. By being authentic, opportunities began to organize around me, leading me on a path I wouldn't have been able to plan. I remember feeling sheer panic as a teenager when family members asked me what I wanted to be when I grew up. I was so small, and the world was so full of possibilities. How could I have known what I wanted to do? So, I chose teaching. That seemed safe and acceptable by traditional standards—including my family's. I got a scholarship to study and went to a school my mentor recommended. I realized when I got there that I was heading down a path of deep regret if I stayed the course. So I leaped away from teaching without knowing what lay ahead, and that curiosity opened doors to discovering something deeply resonant that I could never have had words for then.

I joined a group of women eager to engage in depth psychology and dance therapy, which was a legitimate field in psychology, something I hadn't known until I started the program. I had the incredible fortune of working with a pioneer in the field, mentoring under her and a group of exceptional women for an entire year.

At my first meeting, I felt nervous and intimidated because the other women in the group already knew each other from the first class. The form of dance therapy we practiced involved one person moving in free-form expression while another person witnessed. The person is simply moving their body in whatever way it desires, and that's it.

It's a very simple form of physical expression, and it follows a structure for sharing and giving feedback that honors the mover's experience. The mover shares what they experienced, and the observer shares only if they have permission to do so. Each participant focuses on their own experiences, saying things like, "This is what I saw" and "This is how I felt while watching you." We never say, "This is what you did" or "This is what that meant."

It's a practice centered on honoring inner truths and taking ownership of personal perceptions. This approach was incredibly powerful for me, as I had never engaged in anything like it before.

I paired with someone I didn't know. She was in her 60s, and her movements were a bit clunky. I formed a story in my mind about what I observed. I saw a young Native American man performing a mourning ritual for his deceased partner, the movements emotional and elaborate. I was very moved. I knew deep down that this was probably not her intention with her dance, but it felt like a very clear narrative to me.

When we came back to share, she explained that her movement related to dreams she had about being in her garden, which felt completely unconnected to what I had been thinking. I suddenly felt shy and didn't want to share any longer. Despite my hesitation, they helped me work through my blocks, and I finally shared my observations. It felt somewhat silly, but I expressed what I had seen, and the woman began to cry deeply—tears of release.

She revealed that she had just lost her partner, someone she had cared for over the past couple of years due to their illness. She was attending the group to heal from this loss. The experience was profound for all of us, especially for me. My analytical left brain sought understanding through intellect, yet I found myself seeing and knowing through a different lens altogether. This experience broke something open within me. This practice revealed that the body perceives truth faster than the mind—a realization that would later shape my definition of intuition.

There is so much wisdom in the body, and our big, beautiful conscious mind gets it on a need-to-know basis. I think that's by design. Forgive the computer analogy here—I'm a nerd who studied computer science. The body is like a living database, storing memories, experiences, and patterns that extend beyond individual life events. Some of this information is personal, and some of it is shared.

What psychologist Carl Jung referred to as the "collective unconscious" can be understood as a layer of shared human experience—common beliefs, emotional patterns, and inherited ways of responding to the world that we participate in, whether we're aware of it or not.[2] When people talk about "the field," it's often shorthand for this broader field of information: the invisible but influential web of meaning, memory, and patterning that shapes how we think, feel, and behave.

Embodiment practices, meditation, and movement-based therapies like dance help quiet the analytical mind and bring awareness back into the body, where this information can be accessed more directly. In that state, insight doesn't come from thinking harder—it emerges through sensation, intuition, and felt experience, right when it's actually needed.

I continued to be curious and explore beyond the confines of academia, even while working in the computer science department. When my professor retired, I accepted a position as a student systems administrator, remaining in the department during the day as a computer science student. At night, however, I immersed myself in dance and explored the mind-body connection.

I became interested in Tai Chi and Qigong. Something extraordinary seemed to happen in every class, captivating me and reinforcing the idea that there was something undeniably valuable in this exploration. Through these practices, I experienced subtle energies I had only read about—what I now call Magnetic Intelligence. This is an embodied form of knowing that arises when mind and body come into coherence, allowing for the capacity to sense timing, alignment, and direction through natural resonance rather than analytical control.

We were learning the five elements—Wood, Fire, Earth, Metal, and Water—a traditional Chinese system that maps how energy moves through the body and mirrors cycles in nature, expressed through animal movements known as the Five Animal Frolics. One night, I was having trouble sleeping. I got up and did some movement, thinking it would help me relax. My body started moving spontaneously. I was doing a crane breathing exercise, my arms spreading out and rising above my head and then back down. Only I wasn't doing it. Something in me, some energy source, took over.

The next day, I told my Qigong teacher what happened. He said, "Well, it sounds like you experienced what's known as 'spontaneous qi.' A lot of practitioners spend their entire lives trying to achieve it, and it just happened to you, like beginner's luck." This absolutely

---

2. Jung, C. G. (1959). The Archetypes and the Collective Unconscious (Collected Works, Vol. 9, Part 1). Princeton University Press.

blew my mind beyond anything I thought was possible. It also freaked me out a little. My teacher helped me ground my understanding. I learned to interpret the nature of energy differently.

I continued to engage with that feeling and opened my mind to concepts beyond what I had learned from textbooks. There was a new age bookstore in town where I spent hours browsing. This is where I was introduced to Caroline Myss and many other New Age authors who bridged the gap between our scientific understanding and experiential knowledge. Her work significantly influenced me in this area. Her teachings gave language to what I was discovering experientially: that energy patterns and beliefs shape our health and our path.[3]

The more I practiced yoga, meditation, and Qigong, the more I saw how the mind and body communicate through sensation and rhythm. I noticed that when I quieted the analytical mind, awareness expanded in a way that felt both intelligent and deeply compassionate. It was like discovering that the same field I had been studying in cognitive psychology was alive inside me. This realization blurred the line between observer and observed—what I once approached through research, I was now living through experience.

In my senior year, I continued to follow my intuition, which I referred to as "following my yes." I encountered a class titled "Consciousness and Symbols," taught by the dean of the Department of Anthropology, who specialized in Javanese culture. In this class, we explored how humans create meaning and how the symbols in our lives guide our subconscious beliefs. We examined these processes and how they happen organically due to the brain's structure.

This endeavor aligned closely with my original passion for cognitive psychology, where we focused on language, language processing, and how the brain interprets symbols and synchronicities. We studied influential thinkers like Carl Jung and Claude Lévi-Strauss, who helped shape our understanding of the modern mind. This class provided me with the perfect environment to synthesize everything I had learned throughout my educational journey, as well as my interests in dance, mind-body modalities, yoga, Tai Chi, Qigong, and dance therapy.

---

3. Myss, C. (1996). Anatomy of the Spirit: The Seven Stages of Power and Healing. Harmony Books.

For the first time, I saw my inner and outer worlds aligning—symbols, movement, and science all reflecting the same organizing intelligence.

I was fascinated by how social symbols, gestures, and language become embedded in our neural networks and how collective belief systems can literally shape perception. Studying these cross-cultural frameworks helped me realize that consciousness is not just personal but relational. It lives in the space between us, in the cues, rituals, and archetypes that hold society together.

That class opened a door for me. I began seeing Jung's archetypes not just as metaphors but as energetic realities that could be felt and moved through the body. What we called "intuition" in psychology felt to me like a bridge between these worlds—the nervous system translating symbolic information from the unconscious into perception.

That exploration became the focus of my senior thesis. I titled it "The Thinking Body," sharing my experiences with dance therapy and my spontaneous qi. I argued that, due to Western Cartesian beliefs—the philosophical tradition that treats mind and body as separate entities—we often split the two.[4] We often separate the mind and body, but that separation is an illusion. In reality, the mind and body are one. The brain is not the mind; instead, we have a thinking body, and the mind and body are intrinsically connected.

My professor loved my paper and applauded it, saying it could be my life's work. When he asked what I planned to do with it, I replied, "Live my life." That paper was more than a thesis; it became a compass for everything in my life that followed. Much of what felt radical then is now more mainstream. As I researched business intuition, I found that embodied cognition, predictive processing, and intuition research all echoed what I had first sensed in labs and studios years earlier. I often describe these insights as "little doors opening" or "kismet." These synchronicities act like neurons firing, establishing new pathways for personal growth. They represent a spark within you, a part that recognizes your potential and capabilities, attempting to convey this message to your conscious mind through signs, symbols, and these moments of affirmation.

I also connect this idea to the concept of having a blueprint for success. Reflecting on my own experiences, I remember feeling intimidated by the opportunities that arose in

---

4. Descartes, R. (1952) Meditations on First Philosophy (originally published 1641).

my life. For instance, I would have never thought of attending that dance audition on my own. Despite lacking formal training, the woman conducting the audition saw something in me. If my friend hadn't invited me, I often wonder how different my life would be now.

It's those little places along the way where life shows you a bigger picture than you see yourself, and those small connections begin to form.

By the time I graduated, I no longer saw science and spirit as opposites—they were both languages describing the same mystery. What came next was learning to live from that truth.

Looking back, I can see that this period marked the first time I consciously partnered with mystery—sensing that intuition was not magic but a natural function of consciousness. Each "yes" I followed strengthened that connection, teaching me that science and spirit were not opposites but complementary languages describing the same intelligence.

My Scientific Doorway Into Intuition

When I was a research assistant in visual perception, I designed an experiment we named SHPOT, short for Shelley Spot. This experiment was a series of visual perception studies focused on spots of various shapes and sizes.

We showed participants an image with numerous spots for a duration shorter than 500 milliseconds—just a brief flash. We chose this interval because we know the speed at which information travels along neurons in the brain. By displaying the spots for such a short time, we ensured that the participants' conscious minds wouldn't have enough time to process the information; instead, it engaged their pre-cognitive processing.

After the initial display, we presented them with a single dot and asked, "Was this spot in the original group? Yes or No?" Their responses were essentially guesses. They couldn't accurately recall whether the spot was there or not, as they didn't have time to examine and memorize all the different spots shown to them.

We ran this experiment hundreds of times with participants. Despite the guesses, the analysis of the data revealed something interesting. While the participants' conscious minds were guessing, they weren't completely uninformed. They had an understanding of whether the single spot matched the average size of the largest and smallest spots present in the original group.

What we discovered was that their brains were effectively calculating an average, and storing that information subconsciously. This study aimed to enhance our understanding of how people perceive visual cues, with applications in sonar and radar technology, MRI technology, and other areas in computer science and artificial intelligence.

At that time, artificial intelligence wasn't widely understood, making it an exciting field of exploration. In my experience, I've realized that people often believe they don't know things when, in reality, they're processing information on a subconscious level even before their conscious minds become aware of it.

The entire field of visual perception and our understanding of the mind's workings in relation to artificial intelligence are referred to as "multiple parallel processing." This concept reflects how the brain functions. Neurons in the brain work together to synthesize information; different sections of the brain are continuously processing data and relaying it to other neurons for further synthesis.

For me, this idea brings up the interplay between mind and body. There's a notion of "woo-woo" intuition, which can be understood as knowing something without understanding how you know it. In other words, the system knew before the self "knew." This ties into folk wisdom, the idea that intuition is essentially precognitive processing.

We receive information through subtle cues. With my deeper understanding of consciousness and symbols, I believe we're constantly decoding these cues from each other and our environment into meaningful insights. This understanding has become a fundamental principle in my view of intuition.

As someone whose expertise lies in this area, I've realized that my perspective on intuition differs from many others, stemming from my direct experiences. This definition of intuition has been integral to my work in business alchemy.

Intuition as Navigation

Intuition is often misunderstood as something mystical or irrational. I prefer a different metaphor: intuition is like cartography. A map is not the territory. We can design strategies and build plans, but the landscape of real life always contains variables we cannot fully anticipate. Intuition allows us to navigate that terrain by integrating subtle cues the conscious mind may overlook.

Research in cognitive science supports this view. The brain continuously processes information through multiple parallel pathways, rapidly synthesizing sensory input, memory, and environmental signals before conscious reasoning catches up. Studies of visual perception show that the brain can extract statistical summaries from complex scenes—such as the average size or orientation of objects—within fractions of a second, even when individuals cannot consciously report the details of what they saw.[5] This capacity reflects a broader pattern of rapid, nonconscious pattern recognition that underlies intuitive decision-making.[6]

5. Alvarez, G. A. (2011). Representing multiple objects as an ensemble enhances visual cognition. Trends in Cognitive Sciences, 15(3), 122–131. https://doi.org/10.1016/j.tics.2011.01.003

6. Gigerenzer, G., & Gaissmaier, W. (2011). Heuristic decision making. Annual Review of Psychology, 62, 451–482. Klein, G. (1998). Sources of power: How people make decisions. MIT Press.

Working Definition of Intuition

For the purpose of developing business intuition, I use the following working definition:

Intuition is the brain's ability to synthesize information through multiple parallel processes—simultaneously integrating signals from the senses, memory, emotional cues, and the environment to generate insight before the conscious mind can fully articulate the reasoning behind it.

In cognitive psychology, parallel processing refers to the brain's ability to analyze different features of incoming stimuli at the same time. In vision, for example, the brain separates information about color, motion, shape, and depth, processes each of these streams simultaneously, and then integrates them into a coherent perception.[7] The result is a unified experience that appears instantaneous, even though multiple neural systems are working together behind the scenes.

When this capacity is cultivated, it supports mental flexibility, adaptability, and decision-making under uncertainty. What we often call intuition is simply the system knowing before the self knows—the brain integrating information faster than conscious reasoning can track.

7. Treisman, A. M., & Gelade, G. (1980). A feature-integration theory of attention. Cognitive Psychology, 12(1), 97–136. https://doi.org/10.1016/0010-0285(80)90005-5

Chapter Two

The Soft Pivot

As I approached the end of my senior year in college, I had no clear idea of what I wanted to do after graduation. Despite having had many profound experiences, they didn't seem to translate into a specific job opportunity.

I learned of an opening for a systems administrator at the Environmental Protection Agency (EPA). It was the late '90s, a time when simply having any computer experience made you highly employable. I accepted the position at the EPA because I didn't know what else I was going to do. What followed was far from ideal. I found myself sitting in rush-hour traffic in the Research Triangle Park area of Raleigh-Durham, North Carolina, commuting an hour and a half each way to my job. I absolutely hated it. The days felt long before they even began.

In my first week, a coworker contracted a rare case of spinal meningitis and passed away. The experience shook me. It made the environment feel unsafe in a way I couldn't fully explain, but couldn't ignore.

The combination of that health scare, the grueling nine-to-five, and the commute made it clear I couldn't continue in that role. Within weeks, I began sending out my resume for tech support positions and was contacted by another employer, an opportunity that felt different from the start. This company specialized in spreadsheet software for global clients like NASA, Saudi Arabia, and the state of Alaska—organizations that managed vast amounts of data and required sophisticated spreadsheets to analyze them. They needed a tech support person to serve as a liaison between these entities and their small startup company.

I accepted the role. It was an enjoyable and dynamic environment, and the pay was good. There were five or six employees total, and I had the opportunity to work with the founder of the company, who developed the software, as well as the software engineer who coded everything. We collaborated with brilliant people tackling fascinating and complex challenges on an international scale.

However, a few months in, the woman whom I replaced reached out to me and confessed that she left due to financial issues and had been having trouble getting paid. This news panicked me. Around the same time, my former boss at the Department of Computer Science at UNC contacted me to inform me that a full-time position had opened up. I was ecstatic at the prospect. I took the job at the same place I had worked as an undergraduate, but now I was a full-time employee. It was a great job with good pay and excellent benefits.

About a year into the job, one of my best friends from high school, Paxton, invited me to fulfill our long-held dream of moving to New York. He had just graduated from Yale and was eager to make the move. So, I packed up everything I owned in North Carolina. My boyfriend, Ben, who I had only been dating for a couple of months at that point, helped me with the packing. I gave my notice at work. My colleagues were sad to see me go but excited for me to pursue my dream.

Paxton and I rented a U-Haul truck and loaded it with all of our belongings, including my cat in a small carrier. He already had a job and an apartment lined up in the city, so I didn't have to worry about any logistics. He took care of everything. He had mentioned previously that his father was dealing with health issues, and I had asked him a few times if it was the right moment to move, given the circumstances. He assured me that we were going, regardless.

We drove for 15 hours from North Carolina to New York, parked the U-Haul in a lot in Hell's Kitchen, then took the subway to the realtor's office in Midtown to collect our keys. We were ready to start this new chapter. When we arrived at the office, the realtor looked puzzled. He informed us that the apartment wasn't ready. The renovations weren't yet finished, and it would be another couple of months before we could move in.

We were completely clueless about how real estate works in New York. Now, having lived in New York for 26 years, I can laugh at our naivete. We weren't used to all the red tape of navigating NYC real estate, having experienced nothing like this in North Carolina.

Hoping to take action, I suggested that we speak to the building manager. Maybe they would let us move in anyway. So, we took the subway to the apartment. When we arrived, we found ourselves in a very sketchy area. There were piles of garbage stacked up high on the sidewalks and rats were running everywhere. We walked to the apartment building and knocked on the door of the superintendent.

When he opened the door, we asked if we could see the apartment. He first took us to the basement to show us that the kitchen appliances had arrived but hadn't been installed yet. The apartment itself was gutted; they hadn't even put up walls to conceal the pipes. I could see where someone had taken a crowbar to the door frame to break in. This definitely did not strike me as a safe building. Clearly, it was not going to be a place we could move into right away.

Determined not to give up, I suggested that we look at other apartments and try to find temporary housing. Throughout the process, it became clear that Paxton did not have a job or money. In hindsight, I realized that my instincts—that he shouldn't have moved because his father was sick—were probably correct. He was a bit overwhelmed and not thinking effectively, which had led to this misstep. We tried our best to find an alternative living situation. Meanwhile, we were sleeping in the U-Haul, and my poor cat was confined to the small carrier. Every day, we would take her out to give her food and water. I loved that cat; she was a real trooper.

We really tried our best to find an alternative living situation, but after a few days, we realized that this dream of living in New York just wasn't going to happen. Neither of us had a job, and we needed one to apply for an apartment. I called Ben and said, "We're coming back home."

There was one small problem. We couldn't drive back in the U-Haul because we rented it for one-way only. So, we had to find a new U-Haul. The only one we could find in all of New York City was much smaller than the one we'd arrived in.

There we were, in the middle of an outdoor parking lot in Hell's Kitchen, unpacking everything from the large U-Haul and trying to Tetris all our stuff back into the smaller one. By the end, I jokingly suggested, "You know, I think we should open a moving company when we get back to North Carolina. We're really good at this."

We piled back into the smaller U-Haul and hit the road. I was really perplexed about what to do next. I had quit my job and moved out of my apartment. I took a few months to sort myself out and decided I still wanted to pursue my true passion: dance.

Ben and I were doing well, and I realized I didn't have to leave North Carolina to be happy. I found a part-time job as a systems administrator in a research center at the university so that I could focus on dance. The arrangement worked well for a while until my boss came into my office to tell me they had a full-time position open, working on a web-based data collection project with a different immediate supervisor. My resume had landed on his desk, since it was already on file with the university, and he thought I might be interested.

He asked if I wanted to interview for the full-time position, and I thought, *Sure, why not? Let's see what happens.* I went into the interview and essentially told my potential supervisor, "Look, I have a life, and I want to dance. My focus and priority have always been clear, and I know I'm good at what I do. I won't stick to the traditional nine-to-five hours, but I assure you that I will produce the same quality of work, if not better, during the hours I am present."

Looking back, it's surprising that I expressed my needs so assertively in a job interview. I suppose I felt I had nothing to lose; I knew who I was and what I wanted. The interviewer, impressed, banged his fist on the desk, pointed at me, and said, "You're hired."

That's how I started working full-time again, this time as a web designer and web applications programmer. I stayed there for two and a half years. I excelled at my job and enjoyed a flexible schedule, which allowed me to work part-time managing a yoga studio. I had the opportunity to work with incredible yoga teachers from across the country, and I delved deeply into my understanding of yoga. I took more dance classes. I even joined a local dance company and choreographed my own work. I started getting paid for my performances and participated in amazing local shows at museums and gala events while also contributing to the works of others.

It was truly a wonderful time in my life. But near the end of 1999, challenges arose. There was a significant scandal at the yoga studio, leading to a breakdown in my relationship with the studio owner. I felt betrayed by my friend, who was also my roommate, and a few others in my life. And then Ben announced he was relocating to Michigan to finish his Ph.D. Things felt like they were falling apart. I faced a dilemma: should I stay in NC to further my successful career, move to Michigan and get married, or should I take a leap into the unknown and try again at fulfilling my dream of moving to NYC?

Around this time, I was studying under some of the top yoga instructors in the U.S. A guest instructor visited the studio one weekend. We clicked immediately. He came to the studio regularly to host workshops, and a few of us worked closely with him, forming a deep bond. We discovered we had similar backgrounds, particularly regarding our families, which brought us even closer. As I spent more time with him, he began mentoring me to become a yoga teacher in the lineage in which he was trained. Based in New York, he was known as a yoga teacher to the stars and operated a studio just outside the city.

Paxton also lived in New York—he had made the move successfully this time. I planned a visit to see him one weekend. But when I arrived, he ghosted me. He did not show up to pick me up at the airport and didn't return any of my calls. Not knowing where else to turn, I used a payphone—this was before cell phones, when it cost a quarter to make a call—to reach out to my mentor, who came to pick me up. We ended up spending the entire weekend practicing yoga in his studio. I noticed a book on his bookshelf titled *The Thinking Body*.[1] It amazed me because I had a personal connection to the phrase, believing I had coined it in relation to my life purpose when I wrote my senior thesis in college. Intrigued, I asked him about the book.

He explained that it was written by Mabel Todd, a dancer who had suffered a spinal cord injury. Doctors had told her she would never walk again, but she made a miraculous recovery. In her thesis, she proposed that the body has consciousness and that she could actually communicate with her cells. She could communicate with her organs. Her journey of self-healing was incredibly profound to me.

I felt an immediate connection to this remarkable individual, who I later discovered was the founder of a movement process called ideokinesis. This concept revolves around the idea that the body possesses its own mind—the thinking body. The synchronicity of her book being the title of my thesis and discovering this book while working with my mentor felt significant—a message of affirmation that I was on the right track and needed to keep

1. Todd, M. E. (2008). The Thinking Body: A Study of the Balancing Forces of Dynamic Man. Gestalt Journal Press. (Original work published 1937).

going. It was like finding a little breadcrumb, a sign from my spirit indicating that I needed to let go of doubt, trust the synchronicities, and align more fully with the next step of my path.

In the back of my mind, I had always wanted to return to New York to fulfill my unachieved dream. I was now a much more experienced dancer, had received extensive training, and had built multiple connections in the city. I had just finished a summer at the American Dance Festival in Durham, North Carolina, where I worked with numerous artists and choreographers. Many of them were artists from New York.

Though I had already experienced one New York-related failure, I was starting to believe that something good could happen. While working and performing in North Carolina, I always wondered if I could make money from dancing. Could I elevate my performances from a hobby to something more substantial?

Meanwhile, I heard from Paxton, and he offered me a place to stay. He lived in an apartment in the city and said, "I really owe you. Why don't you come? You can stay with me for as long as you need to get settled." Until then, I thought I was never going to be successful. I was doing all the "right things" I was "supposed to do," but it felt like I was living someone else's life, following someone else's idea of what I should be doing. I was good at my work but sensed it was time to tip the scales and pursue my dream. It truly felt like a "now or never" moment, and I was ready to take a leap. I gave my notice at my job and moved to New York in September 2000.

At this point in my life, I was beginning to realize that I needed to let go of some of the conditioning I had received and start trusting myself more. When I chose myself, opportunities started to come into view—not because they suddenly appeared, but because I was finally able to recognize them.

I had accepted a set of beliefs without questioning them—that this is just how life is, that you must do drudgery work to make a living, and that you should give up on your dreams. Yet my conditioning was gradually changing, and something within me was beginning to thaw. At that point, with a growing sense of what felt most aligned, I was willing to take a chance, even if it meant facing the possibility of failure.

That realization raised a deeper question: what actually defines success? Each person has their own unique blueprint for success and their own way of manifesting it. I could feel myself beginning to access mine more fully.

Synchronicity and Peak Performance

Synchronicity plays a fascinating role in peak performance, particularly during periods of transition when direction is not yet fully formed but alignment is beginning to emerge. Athletes, artists, and professionals often describe being "in the zone," a state in which actions feel timely, decisions come more easily, and external circumstances begin to organize in supportive ways.

Psychological research on flow describes a state of deep absorption in which attention is fully engaged in the present moment.[2] One of the defining conditions of flow is the balance between challenge and skill: The task must be demanding enough to fully engage attention but not so overwhelming that it pushes the nervous system into sympathetic overdrive, a stress response, where anxiety and reactivity begin to override clarity. When the level of challenge is well matched to an individual's capacity, attention stabilizes and effort becomes more fluid. If the challenge is too low, boredom emerges. If it is too high, the system shifts toward stress and fragmentation rather than coherence.[3]

During these states, activity in parts of the prefrontal cortex associated with self-monitoring decreases, allowing for faster, more fluid responses.[4] Rather than overanalyzing each step, individuals are able to respond to what is unfolding with greater precision and adaptability.

---

2. Csikszentmihalyi, M. (1990). Flow: The psychology of optimal experience. Harper & Row.

3. Nakamura, J., & Csikszentmihalyi, M. (2009). Flow theory and research. In S. J. Lopez & C. R. Snyder (Eds.), Oxford handbook of positive psychology (2nd ed., pp. 195–206). Oxford University Press.

4. Dietrich, A. (2004). Neurocognitive mechanisms underlying the experience of flow. Consciousness and Cognition, 13(4), 746–761. https://doi.org/10.1016/j.concog.2004.07.002 https://doi.org/10.1016/j.concog.2004.07.002

What is often less discussed is how this internal shift changes the way we interact with our environment. As attention stabilizes and internal conflict decreases, people become more responsive to opportunities, relationships, and information that were previously overlooked or dismissed. The environment itself has not necessarily changed, but the capacity to recognize and act on what is available has.

From this perspective, synchronicity can be understood as the meeting point between internal alignment and external timing. Research in decision science suggests that experienced decision-makers rely on rapid, nonconscious pattern recognition to guide action in complex environments.[5,6] When this capacity is supported by focused attention and reduced cognitive noise, individuals are more likely to notice meaningful connections and respond to them effectively.

In peak performance states, this creates the experience of events "lining up." Encounters feel timely, resources appear when needed, and decisions unfold with a sense of coherence rather than force. These moments often reinforce confidence, deepen engagement, and further stabilize the conditions that support high-level performance.

---

5. Gigerenzer and Gaissmaier, "Heuristic Decision Making." Klein, *Sources of Power*.

6. Klein, G. (1998). *Sources of power: How people make decisions*. MIT Press.

Chapter Three

From Hustle to Healing

When I first arrived in New York, I felt a sense of kismet; doors seemed to open effortlessly for me. An internet startup company in New Jersey was trying to recruit me, but I kept insisting, "I'm here to be a dancer, not a programmer." The recruiter wouldn't give up and eventually proposed that I could work four days a week for a full-time salary. I agreed because this arrangement seemed like an excellent way to support myself and take classes in the city. I also wanted to rent my own apartment, which meant building a steady, substantial income to make it possible.

Meanwhile, I felt excited to be living close enough to audition for my performance group in Boston and dancing for the company despite being away for so long. Shortly after settling into my new apartment, I received a call from the startup company in New Jersey informing me that they were closing down. Suddenly, I was responsible for rent, commuting on weekends to Boston to finish the season, and trying to navigate auditions with no income. I was out of work for about four months and started working nights part-time at JPMorgan Chase on Wall Street to support myself.

Around the same time, my tumultuous friendship with Paxton came to a crashing end. Losing my once lifelong friend added to the sense of abrupt endings that marked that period.

That first year was filled with intense financial stress. My first anniversary in the city was 9/11. That morning, as I was getting ready to leave for dance class, my mother called and told me not to go out. I turned on the TV and watched everything unfold. Many people I knew left New York after 9/11, fracturing my support network. I debated whether to stay, but ultimately decided to remain. To afford the city, I needed a roommate.

Angela, a dancer who had just completed her master's of fine arts degree in Michigan and was new to the city, moved in. She helped me get a job where she worked, a large movement center that rented rehearsal space and hosted dance classes. After a few classes together, she approached me with an offer to join her dance company. It was my first opportunity to perform regularly and rehearse consistently in the city. I participated in festivals in New York and traveled for performances.

Angela enrolled in a Pilates teacher training program and asked me to be her practice student. Since I had studied Pilates in North Carolina, I happily accepted the free sessions. When it came time for her exam, I served as her test subject and met Kelly, a master Pilates teacher and respected bodyworker. During my first assessment, Kelly lightly touched my hand and started describing my health in detail. I hadn't said a word. I was stunned. Angela passed her exam, and I gained a mentor. Kelly invited me to become her scholarship student and apprentice.

In the aftermath of 9/11, the artistic community felt bonded. I eventually left my Wall Street job to commit fully to movement and dance. A week before I was set to begin my own Pilates teacher training, I suffered a serious knee injury, tearing my ACL on a trampoline.

After hours at the movement center, we would set up a large Olympic trampoline. It was exhilarating and addictive. One night, exhausted after working and dancing all day, I agreed to jump with someone else. During a double jump, I felt my knee crack and crumple. The injury required reconstructive surgery and a year of rehabilitation.

After surgery, I began my Pilates teacher training with an intensive physical therapy and rehabilitation component. Going through that process as an injured person transformed my understanding of healing. I became a case study in my own recovery.

While I was learning about healing through my training, I returned to work just a week after surgery—hobbling through the studio with a cane and leg brace and navigating the subway without giving myself time to heal. My usual methods of achieving goals started to fail. I quickly learned that the more I pushed, the harder it was to recover. In New York, I had operated with a superhuman mentality, expecting my body to perform beyond its limits. It had served me before, but it stopped working. Even as I became skilled at helping others rehabilitate, I struggled myself.

As I invested in my own healing, my abilities as a practitioner deepened. Clients often told me that when I touched them, it felt different. One dancer I worked with struggled with a particular exercise and asked why. I replied with the name of a disease I had never consciously learned. The words slipped out unexpectedly. She got spooked and stopped working with me. Years later, I ran into her and learned she had been diagnosed with that exact condition.

This experience felt like a continuation of the mind-body exploration I had begun in college, now deepening through intuitive, embodied awareness in new and unexpected ways.

During my training, I noticed *The Thinking Body* on Kelly's bookshelf. I learned that her mentor, Irene Dowd, was a student of ideokinesis and taught anatomy and kinesiology at Juilliard. Eventually, I studied with Irene myself, completing a year-long intensive in anatomy, kinesiology, and movement sequences designed to awaken body consciousness.

Over the years, ongoing knee issues limited my ability to dance the way I initially envisioned. Despite outward signs of success, I struggled to feel positive. Something had disrupted the vision I once held for my future. I began to carry a quiet belief that things simply didn't work out for me, yet at the same time, I held a paradoxical hope that I would somehow find my way back to health. There was an inner tension between these two narratives—one shaped by disappointment and another that refused to let go of the possibility of recovery.

When I visited my family, conversations often returned to practicality and the importance of keeping a stable day job. Those remarks, likely meant as encouragement toward security, quietly reinforced the growing sense that my path had veered off course.

At the same time, I had built a life that ran entirely on momentum. Slowing down didn't feel like an option, so I kept moving forward even when the direction no longer made sense.

Looking back now, I can see how much that pattern shaped the way I approached challenges. It would eventually become one of the most important lessons of my work: the difference between forcing outcomes through pressure and allowing change to emerge through alignment.

As I continued on my journey, I found myself managing a large space, teaching full-time, and feeling like a vital part of an amazing community. After my rehabilitation, I continued to jump on the trampoline. A friend of mine, Lindsey, often came to jump with her friend Peter, and the community vibe was wonderful. Eventually, I was invited to become a teacher trainer in their Pilates teacher training program.

Throughout this time, I had been riding a wave of positivity and flow. I wasn't overthinking. I was teaching Pilates classes at DanceSpace, one of the largest professional dance training centers in New York, and running their works-in-progress performance series and one of the largest dance studios in New York. I enjoyed dancing and choreographing my own work. Even amidst all of this, that feeling that something was off, almost as if my life wasn't entirely my own, still lingered a small bit.

I had already decided that I didn't want to be a Broadway dancer or perform in a major dance company. I wasn't actively auditioning or seeking a spot in a company. Yet, opportunities to dance in smaller projects and perform in ways that aligned with my goals continued to present themselves.

I was the rehearsal director for my friend's dance company and involved in many amazing projects. There was a sense that things were opening up for me, but whenever an opportunity arose, some disruption seemed to occur that prevented me from building a strong foundation. Shortly after I received the offer to join the Pilates teacher training program, I had a falling-out with the owner. He was generally upset with the management of the space, which had little to do with me, even though I managed the Pilates department. It seemed he was navigating larger business challenges, and I found myself caught in the crossfire.

I started to adapt to the idea that I shouldn't get my hopes up or desire too much, as things often didn't work out for me. Opportunities were coming my way, yet I still questioned what I truly wanted. What was I trying to create? Was it enough to simply go with the flow, or did I need to focus on building a stronger foundation?

A lot of the disruptions in my life mirrored the feeling that I had one foot in and one foot out, moving between several worlds at once, but not fully planted in any of them. Even my injury represented this uncertainty. I started to ask myself where I truly wanted to stand.

I became more invested in my Pilates teaching and moved to another studio. It was during this time that people started reaching out to me with business partnership opportunities.

One of my Pilates students was a successful dancer with the Rockettes and an excellent Pilates instructor. We had worked together on her lower back injuries, and our friendship deepened as we became colleagues. She approached me about opening a studio together, and I was thrilled at the prospect. However, just as we began discussing our plans, she suddenly disappeared. Later, I found out she had experienced a major health issue that required significant surgery and rehabilitation over the course of a year and a half, which thwarted our plans.

A second opportunity arose when someone I knew mentioned that her instructor was looking for someone to rent space from her new business. I met with her, and while I was excited about the opportunity, I struggled to envision making the leap from my comfortable teaching role with a full schedule in one part of the city to starting a business in a completely different area.

I thought, *I don't want to say no, but I'm not sure how to say yes.*

So I went home and performed a manifesting meditation, expressing my strong desire to break free from working for others and to fulfill my lifelong dream of owning my own business. As soon as I finished the meditation and opened my email, I found a message from the woman. She had spoken with a colleague about my interest in the space, and the colleague was fully on board. The three of us would be working together to bring this plan to fruition.

That experience was truly amazing. I felt supported, especially because the person joining me was a longtime friend and colleague whom I had worked with for years.

I was relocating to a different part of the city, and I didn't bring many of my clients with me. In our excitement, I think we all jumped in without fully nailing down the details. They had made other arrangements regarding the schedule, which meant that what I had envisioned for the structure didn't end up working out. There was an expectation that I would simply make it all work, even as they focused on their own needs.

To survive, I ended up working twelve-hour days, six days a week, for nearly two years. I went into "do mode," which was exhausting but also incredibly productive. I became quite skilled at what I was doing. As much as I hoped this would be the big launch of my own business, partnering with others, I struggled to keep up the pace and adapt to a schedule that didn't work for me.

During this time, I also engaged more deeply with my manifesting meditations. My partner and I found a discarded window frame on the streets of Brooklyn and took it home. He turned it into a dry-erase board that we hung in our living room. Before long, it was filled with to-do lists and all the tasks we were working on.

One birthday, when we were having a party and had cleaned up the apartment, I erased everything from the board and wrote "ABUNDANCE" in all capital letters. For fun, I had everyone do a dance ritual to call in the intention. That moment turned into an annual ritual for me, where each year I would choose a new word to define the coming year.

Around that time, the busyness in my life took shape and fit into the container I had been asking for. What had once felt chaotic organized itself into something more sustainable.

One day, my partner burst through the door, completely wide-eyed. "Oh my God, my life is forever changed, Shelley," he said. "I just experienced the most incredible thing!"

My trampoline friend Lindsey had just given him a consciousness-based, integrative energy healing session. Afterward, he rushed home, breathless, to tell me I had to try it.

I started going to Lindsey's apartment once a week to receive sessions of my own. Lindsey was able to talk to my body, and my body told her what it needed to be balanced. I had been on overdrive for so long, but after just a few weeks of those sessions, my stress levels dropped significantly. I noticed that situations that previously stressed me out no longer had the same grip on me. I began to feel a sense of space and open possibilities in my life.

Energy healing focuses on the consciousness of the body, much like Mabel Todd's work in ideokinesis. The idea that the body's systems communicate and store memories that influence health resonated deeply with me. It was fascinating to witness this synchronicity. Suddenly, the different parts of my life that had once felt separate—dance, healing, psychology, and my academic background in cognition—converged. For the first time, I felt I had a cohesive framework that allowed me to integrate all of those pieces into one coherent practice.

As this new sense of integration was emerging, I noticed a curious pattern: when situations felt beyond my control, support and resources often appeared in unexpected ways.

One morning, I had to wake up really early to fly out and see my family, and I didn't want to go. I was not looking forward to this trip. Every time I came back from visiting them, I felt horrible, as if I had abandoned them and that I was incredibly selfish for pursuing my dreams far away from home.

On top of everything, I was struggling financially. Paying for the trip was going to put a strain on my already tight budget, and I desperately needed the money I was missing out on by not working for the next few days.

Exhausted and full of dread, I hauled my suitcase through the New York City subways to the New Jersey Transit station only to realize I was never going to make it on time. With no money to cover it, I hailed a cab and found myself sounding like a frantic character from a bad action movie: "Step on it!"

Cabs to Newark were expensive, and as the meter approached $125, I watched my resources dwindle and my panic escalate, unsure if I would even make my flight.

The cab dropped me at my terminal. Still dark out and with no one else around, I stepped up to the kiosk only to find there was no record of my flight.

I had gone to the wrong terminal.

Absolutely defeated, I threw up my hands and declared to the empty air, "I give up!" I slumped against the kiosk, burying my forehead in my elbow, near tears.

When I looked up, I saw a book titled *Attitude Is Everything: 10 Life-Changing Steps to Turning Attitude into Action* by Keith Harrell sitting on the counter.

It felt like a direct message from the cosmos.

My attitude was at an all-time low, shaping every action. I wasn't looking forward to the trip, and that resistance was present in every moment. I was also allowing others' opinions about my life choices to impact my ability to experience joy and excitement about what I was doing. That was spilling over into my finances, my energy levels, and my belief in my capacity to create success.

At that moment, every cell in my body shifted. I jumped up, grabbed the book, and got myself to the right terminal, on time, and onto my flight. I devoured every word of that book, finishing it by the time my flight landed.

I ended up having a great trip because I made a conscious choice then and there not to allow anyone to shake my belief in what was possible. My takeaway from the book was that if you know who you are and what you want, you can create a life map to get you there, no matter how long it might take.

The client case studies in that book taught me two things. Some dreams can take a lifetime to come true. Most people aren't willing to do what it takes, either because they're not willing to put the work in or because they are dreaming about something they don't actually want.

That trip really turned my life around. I immediately began a regular gratitude practice, which I now teach to others, and started focusing on taking action toward what I wanted. I gave myself permission to let manifesting my dreams be a lifelong journey and to do the deep work of getting clear about what I do and don't want. I saw my life through a new lens.

Much of the negativity and sense of failure I had felt came from relying too heavily on willpower without clear direction. I was also in a relationship that wasn't working, and instead of confronting that reality, I was sublimating my frustrations into my career. It was during this process that my relationship fell apart.

Previously, I wouldn't have been okay with the relationship ending. It was a toxic dynamic that reinforced the belief that leaving meant I was giving up. I was putting his needs above my own and carrying the responsibility for the relationship's success on my shoulders. I saw how I was enabling his dysfunction and that by stepping back from the savior role, I was allowing something new to happen. Through the changes I made within myself, the relationship ended organically.

I decided to transition from energy healing client to practitioner. I was able to develop a thriving practice where people often referred their most challenging clients to me. Clients told their friends about me and started calling me a "people whisperer."

"Just go have a session with Shelley. I can't explain it—just go!"

That's when everything really started to take off. I realized the pieces of my life were coming together, and I was invited to start hosting continuing education classes in energy healing locally in New York City. There had once been a large community, but many of the key individuals moved away, creating an opening for someone to take on the role. Given my strong interest in continuing my studies, I stepped in, and it turned out to be an amazing time. I hosted courses year-round, allowing me to meet people from all over the world and connect with a global community interested in consciousness. It was phenomenal.

This marked a turning point in how I understood intuition—a time of rapid learning and expansion. I actively developed intuition as a professional skill, learning to recognize, trust, and act on it in real time with clients. I was no longer just intellectually or mystically tuning into it.

I was deeply engaged in this work, and through the community, new opportunities continued to arise. A colleague approached me about joining a medical practice with integrative healthcare practitioners. We worked alongside holistic chiropractors, psychiatrists, massage therapists, and acupuncturists, all within one integrated space, collaborating across disciplines. It marked a significant evolution in my work, expanding into leadership and professional development in a way that felt both elevated and deeply rewarding—a natural culmination of everything I had been building.

Initially, I agreed to join the practice to have a space for energy healing sessions. The studio where I'd been working recently moved and shifted its focus to fitness, leaving no room for healing work. That meant I would be split between two locations: the old practice and the new.

However, once I signed the lease and stood in the new space, something shifted within me. I knew this was a place where I could bring all of my offerings together and serve all of my clients under one roof.

At that moment, I knew I needed to step into my vision and follow my dream. I had been thinking about it for many years. I even had unsent drafts of business announcements sitting in my email, dating back to 2004 and 2005. Now, in 2012, I was finally ready.

I returned to my studio and spoke with my dear friends, who had supported my growth for six years. It felt clear that the chapter we had shared there was coming to a close, and I told them I was ready to step out on my own.

Years of significant breakthroughs alongside moments of collapse led me to this moment. This journey opened me up to my gifts and set me on my path. My journey had been disrupted by my injury, which highlighted the tension I felt between my career, dance, and wellness. Ultimately, it guided me to focus on my health and deepen my understanding of wellness from a rehabilitation perspective rather than a performance-based one.

Through this experience, I integrated many elements that I had previously compartmentalized. Later, we will explore how these patterns relate to ancestral healing and how I noticed a recurring manifestation pattern: getting very close to achieving something significant, yet it doesn't quite materialize.

I relied on my manifestation practices, which provided small signs and insights along the way. They guided me, but the full realization of my goals was elusive at the time.

The injury forced me to stop my hectic pace of working two jobs while dancing and choreographing. It pushed me to slow down, examine who I was beneath the movement, and begin building a stronger foundation. That interruption activated my gifts. It led to invitations to join practices and eventually positioned me as a standalone practitioner. What felt like a setback became a turning point.

At that point, I was navigating the distinction between destructive and constructive manifestation. Destructive manifestation occurs when we create outcomes from unresolved wounds. The nervous system, shaped by implicit memory and repetition, unconsciously recreates familiar dynamics. Trauma stored in the body seeks resolution through reenactment. We think we are moving forward, but we often find ourselves circling old patterns.[1]

---

1. LeDoux, J. (2002). *Synaptic self: How our brains become who we are*. New York, NY: Viking.

Constructive manifestation begins when awareness interrupts that cycle. Instead of generating outcomes from survival patterns, we make changes that support regulation, coherence, and intentional growth. The energy that once reinforced repetition becomes available for expansion. The injury forced me to make those changes. It required me to shift from creating through pain and into creating from alignment.

That shift became foundational. It shaped how I understood healing, identity, and work.

Intuitive Knowing: The Power of Not Knowing

Many people say, "I'm not good at meditation. I don't know if I'm doing it right." But the whole point of meditation is not knowing. The conscious mind, the one that wants to evaluate and achieve, is precisely the part that must soften for deeper awareness to arise.

In neuroscience, this corresponds to a shift from the analytical, problem-solving networks of the brain to what's known as the observer mind, a state of meta-awareness that allows us to witness experience without getting lost in it. This witnessing activates integration and helps us perceive subtler rhythms: the pulse of emotion, the movement of energy, and the intelligence within sensation.[2]

Earlier in this book, we explored how intuition emerges from the body's ongoing effort to maintain balance. Much of the information shaping our perceptions and decisions is processed continuously beneath conscious awareness. The body is constantly receiving signals—changes in breathing, heart rate, muscle tone, digestion, and other subtle shifts that reflect how we are responding to our environment.[3]

These signals form part of the background processing that informs intuitive awareness. Because homeostatic systems operate faster than deliberate reasoning, intuitive knowing often appears as a sudden recognition. What feels like a flash of insight is frequently the

---

2. Tang, Y., Hölzel, B. K., & Posner, M. I. (2015). The neuroscience of mindfulness meditation. *Nature Reviews. Neuroscience*, 16(4), 213–225. https://doi.org/10.1038/nrn3916

3. Craig, A. D. (2009). How do you feel—now? The anterior insula and human awareness. *Nature Reviews Neuroscience*, 10, 59–70. https://doi.org/10.1038/nrn2555

integration of signals the body has already registered and organized outside conscious attention[4] —an ability that researchers studying decision-making describe as rapid pattern recognition occurring beneath conscious awareness.[5]

Neuroscience continues to illuminate how this process unfolds. Studies using fMRI show that intuitive decision-making activates the insula, a region involved in interoception, or the brain's capacity to detect and interpret internal bodily signals, shaping emotional awareness and the ability to regulate and respond to internal cues with clarity. The brain continuously distributes incoming information across specialized regions and integrates the results before conscious interpretation occurs.

Some researchers believe the claustrum, a crown-like sheet of neurons connecting multiple regions of the brain, may play an important coordinating role in this integration.[6] By linking subconscious processing with conscious awareness, it may help shape the intuitive insights that surface during complex decision-making.

Recent work by Carvalho and Damasio adds another layer to this picture. Their research suggests that the interoceptive nervous system communicates through slow-conducting, unmyelinated fibers and even non-synaptic chemical signaling. These pathways generate the qualitative, felt dimension of experience that later becomes emotion, intuition, and meaning. In this way, consciousness of feelings emerges when the brain interprets the body's homeostatic signals—transforming physiology into awareness.[7]

When these internal communication systems are functioning clearly, they support emotional regulation, boundary-setting, and discernment. We can sense the difference

---

4. Watson, K., & D. Kahneman. (2011). Thinking, Fast and Slow. New York, NY: Farrar, Straus and Giroux. 499 pages. *Canadian Journal of Program Evaluation*, 26(2), 111–113. https://doi.org/10.3138/cjpe.26.010

5. Klein, G. (1998). *Sources of power: How people make decisions*. MIT Press.

6. Crick, F. C., & Koch, C. (2005). What is the function of the claustrum? *Philosophical Transactions of the Royal Society B: Biological Sciences*, 360(1458), 1271–1279. https://doi.org/10.1098/rstb.2005.1661

7. Carvalho, G. B., & Damasio, A. (2021). Interoception and the origin of feelings: A new synthesis. *BioEssays, 43*(6), e2000261. https://doi.org/10.1002/bies.202000261

between anxiety and genuine misalignment, perceiving nuance without needing to analyze every variable.[8]

When the nervous system is overwhelmed, however, these signals can become harder to interpret. Chronic stress or trauma may disrupt the clarity of internal cues, making intuition feel distant or unreliable. Many people describe difficulty making even simple decisions when their system is in sympathetic overdrive. The signals are still present, but they can become difficult to distinguish from urgency or fear.

This is one reason intuition development often involves practices that calm the nervous system and reduce cognitive noise. As discussed earlier, reflective practices such as meditation, mindfulness, visualization, and energy-based healing approaches can help restore clarity by shifting the brain away from constant problem-solving and toward more integrative modes of awareness.

At a biological level, the body is constantly synchronizing with rhythms we did not invent. The tides, the lunar cycle, and the rise and fall of breath reflect patterns that influence living systems across scales.

Modern chronobiology has begun documenting what many earlier traditions observed intuitively: the human body does not operate in isolation but in relationship with larger environmental rhythms.[9] Lunar light, solar radiation, gravitational forces, and electromagnetic patterns all influence the timing of our internal clocks.[10]

Artificial light, constant connectivity, and around-the-clock productivity can disrupt this natural synchronization. When the body is continually pushed into artificial rhythms, the nervous system often remains in a state of low-grade activation.[11] Under those

---

8. Thayer, J. F., & Lane, R. D. (2009). Claude Bernard and the heart–brain connection: Further elaboration of a model of neurovisceral integration. *Neuroscience & Biobehavioral Reviews, 33*(2), 81–88. https://doi.org/10.1016/j.neubiorev.2008.08.004

9. Roenneberg, T., & Merrow, M. (2016). The circadian clock and human health. *Current Biology, 26*(10), R432–R443. https://doi.org/10.1016/j.cub.2016.04.011

10. Cart, C. (2025). Chronobiology: The dynamic field of rhythm and clock genes. *Institute for Functional Medicine.* https://www.ifm.org/articles/chronobiology-dynamic-field-rhythm-clock-geneshttps://www.ifm.org/articles/chronobiology-dynamic-field-rhythm-clock-genes

11. Foster, R. G., & Kreitzman, L. (2017). *Circadian rhythms: A very short introduction.* Oxford University Press.

conditions, the subtle signals that inform intuition become harder to perceive amid the noise of constant stimulation.

When we create space for the nervous system to recalibrate—even briefly—the body begins to resynchronize with these underlying rhythms. Attention softens, perception widens, and the background processing that informs intuitive awareness becomes easier to recognize. Creativity resurfaces. Insights arrive in ways that do not follow linear reasoning.

From this perspective, mystery is not something to eliminate but something to work with. Much of the information shaping our decisions is processed outside conscious awareness. In complex environments where time and information are limited, experienced decision-makers often rely on this form of rapid pattern recognition to guide action.[12] When we allow space for that processing to unfold, intuition can surface insights that analysis alone cannot generate.[13]

The body becomes the meeting point of the seen and unseen, the conscious and unconscious, the known and the unknowable. Leadership that draws on intuition acknowledges this complexity rather than attempting to control it.

In a world that rewards certainty and speed, the most visionary leaders often do the opposite. They pause. They listen. They create space for the integration of information occurring beneath conscious thought.

Leadership, in this sense, is less about control and more about coherence.

For conscious leaders, mystery is not a problem to manage but a source of insight to partner with. Decisions emerge from resonance rather than reactivity. Innovation arises from intuition rather than fear. Teams align through coherence rather than command.

When leaders learn to work with the quiet intelligence of intuition alongside rational analysis, decision-making becomes both grounded and expansive. Research on expert decision-making suggests that intuitive pattern recognition often becomes most valuable in environments characterized by uncertainty, time pressure, and incomplete

---

12. Gigerenzer, G. (2007). *Gut feelings: The intelligence of the unconscious.* Viking in Penguin Group.

13. Gigerenzer, G., & Gaissmaier, W. (2011). Heuristic decision making. *Annual Review of Psychology, 62*, 451–482. https://doi.org/10.1146/annurev-psych-120709-145346

information.[14] They are no longer relying solely on what can be calculated in advance. They are also listening to the deeper pattern recognition emerging from the system itself.

This capacity—to hold uncertainty without collapsing into control—may be one of the most important leadership skills of our time.

14. Dane, E., & Pratt, M. G. (2007). Exploring intuition and its role in managerial decision making. *Academy of Management Review*, 32(1), 33–54. https://doi.org/10.5465/amr.2007.23463682

Chapter Four

Awakening Business Intuition

There was a moment in my life when I stopped seeing myself as someone destined to fail and began embodying the version of me who could lead and grow and help others to do the same. By challenging the filters of failure I had carried since childhood, I began reclaiming a deeper trust in my instincts and recognizing that the very patterns shaping my struggles were also shaping my business.

It was 2012, and I finally realized a long-held dream: I started my own business, BodyAttune Wellness. I had been cultivating the concept of "BodyAttune" for at least five to ten years. When it came time to officially incorporate, I was thrilled to bring it to life. I made an investment and bought a Pilates machine. My energy healing clients followed me. I was immersed in a community of wellness practitioners, feeling excited about the future.

For the first time, I realized that the work I was doing on my clients and the healing I was receiving might also apply to my business. I started integrating many of the concepts I had learned in college, exploring ideas I had discovered while wandering through New Age bookstores. I worked with archetypes, drawing inspiration from Caroline Myss and Carl Jung, and I understood that my business could operate on a blueprint for health, ensuring its optimal performance. This was just the beginning of my journey.

This was also the first time I considered the idea of business energetics. I saw my business as a living system, an ecosystem shaped by its internal structures, relationships, and purpose, much like the body itself. Just as misalignments in the body create imbalance, unseen energetic or structural blocks within a business can restrict flow and growth. To support my vision, I created a list of people from my life who represented unwavering belief in my success to represent an energetic board of advisors. I was calling for the energy of people who could help me disrupt the limiting patterns that had been running my business up until that point.

I started with my inner circle, those who represent the encouraging energy that kept opening doors for me: My sixth-grade teacher, who encouraged my writing skills and believed in me when I struggled to see my own potential; the cognitive psychology professor, who took a chance and gave me my first academic job; my visual perception mentor, who encouraged me to pursue my passions above academic rigor; and my friend Lindsey, who introduced me to energy healing.

All these individuals were instrumental in my journey. They helped me move forward, especially during times when I believed that success was reserved for others and that I shouldn't expect too much for myself.

In my outer circle, I looked to those in the world who were creating things that resonated with my vision. This included my mentors from various fields of study, as well as inspirational figures like Richard Branson. Although I had no desire to become a billionaire entrepreneur, I admired his ability to continually innovate and learn from every experience. He represented wholehearted belief in success, and my inner and outer circle members were holding that for me since I couldn't hold it for myself. When I finished it, it felt like I had cast a circle. I called it my inner and outer circles, similar to the sacred wheel of archetypes Caroline Myss describes in her book *Sacred Contracts*, where core archetypal energies are intentionally placed around one's life as sources of guidance and accountability. I hadn't consciously framed it that way at the time, but once I saw the parallel, it resonated.

By treating my business as a living, energetic entity, assembling inner and outer circles of support, and challenging the filters of failure I had carried since childhood, I discovered my innate business intuition, reclaimed my power, and stepped into the truth that I was always meant to succeed.

It felt like something shifted. Old patterns surfaced in my interactions with clients and colleagues—conversations and situations that mirrored past habits playing out in real time. They brought up beliefs I'd been holding unconsciously in my body and in my business. I observed these patterns as they emerged and then watched them dissolve. I began to refer to this shedding process as "unwinding." As things unwound, those patterns resolved and no longer showed up within me or my business, like an interference I had released.

One of the most stubborn repeating patterns was experiencing a disruption every time I hit the $50,000 mark in my business. Any time my business approached that number—whether in gross revenue, net profit, savings, or investments—I would immediately hit a wall: a downturn in client engagement, fractures in business relationships or leases, or unexpected expenses and bills.

At the time, I didn't yet understand why this was happening, but I had begun working with a process that helped me access deeper insight around goals, money, and decision-making. I began meditating on the $50,000, asking:

What does this money represent?Why is it significant?Is there anything I can understand better about my current circumstances that would clarify why this number is showing up right now?

Through that inquiry, I saw what had been operating beneath the surface. I was able to identify a limiting belief operating energetically that came from an invisible, arbitrary cap I had from childhood: I could never be more financially successful than my dad. At a young age, that's what I understood his salary to be, and I didn't understand base pay, bonuses, overtime, raises, or even the value of $50,000. I had encoded that amount as an invisible ceiling in my subconscious. Once I unpacked that, I was able to release the limiting belief that my financial success was tied to his in any way.

Once I cast my inner and outer circles, I realized I was reprogramming or repatterning my business to align with what I had set in motion. I included archetypes that represented affirmation, openness, and a resonance with what I aimed to create. All the energy surrounding it began to unwind and realign with what I desired. I realized that my business, even though I was finally standing on my own two feet, had always existed; it was just an experience happening to me.

That little spark I had been feeling all along, those hints of breadcrumbs, suddenly accelerated and catalyzed tremendously. I recognized a recurring theme of being guided toward something greater than I could envision for myself. It all coalesced into an understanding that my business had been demonstrating to me all along: I was asking for too little and misaligned with what I truly wanted to create.

With this realization front and center, better-fitting opportunities came my way, urging me to dream bigger and helping me break free from the habit of keeping myself small for the sake of humility. That unfortunate tendency had limited my ability to make an impact and connect with those who truly needed what I had to offer. I had been doing this work, but it was often under the umbrella of someone else's business or community. Something shifted profoundly in the BizAttune process when I decided to step out on my own.

I started working with this process daily. Each morning, I checked in with my business and asked, "What should I focus on today?" The results were remarkable. I would receive small insights, like reminders that someone needed to be contacted. *Sally is going to miss her appointment at noon,* my inner knowing would tell me. So I would message her, and she would respond, "Oh my goodness, thank you for reminding me. I forgot we had an appointment today."

It had never been so conscious for me before, but once I fully embodied my business and recognized *business intuition* as a real entity, it became clear that this idea of entrepreneurship had been instilled in me from a young age by my father. He taught me that true freedom comes from having your own business, not just in terms of financial freedom, but in transcending the limitations others might impose on you when it comes to your dreams. There's a profound freedom in creating something that perhaps hasn't been created before.

I found myself standing in this newfound space, surrounded by a powerful energy. It was exhilarating and terrifying at the same time, and deep down, I knew I was going to fail. I just knew it.

I had been dreaming about this for so long. When the opportunity arose to join that integrative practice alongside other holistic practitioners and run my own independent business, it almost didn't feel real. I needed to just take the leap, fail, and move on with my life. That realization was 100 percent my inspiration to go for it, to stop leaving my announcement in the drafts folder, to face whatever reactions came my way, and to acknowledge that I might be terrible at running a business. I thought, *I don't have a head for business, I can't stay organized; I'll fail and then I can go back to working in a studio or find something else to do.* But the opposite happened. I became wildly successful.

I remember that, in the practice, all the practitioners would collaborate, referring clients to one another. I was working with one of the chiropractors who was giving me an adjustment. He asked me, "How do you do it?"

I replied, "Do what?"

He said, "I see people coming in and out of your space all day long. You're fully booked from open to close, without any breaks. When we were in chiropractic school, we were taught that was the goal, but I haven't quite gotten there yet. How did you achieve this?"

I laughed because it was the first time I had worked somewhere with regular nine-to-five office hours. I told him, "This is the slowest I've ever been." And that was the truth. This was the slowest I'd ever been but also the most stable in my time, finances, and ability to have a personal life. I shared that with him and encouraged him to let go of the idea that overwork equals achievement and instead focus on strategies that would support the business he wanted rather than the business he was told he was supposed to have.

My two years of working 12-hour days, six days a week, feeling like I was in boot camp, had prepared me to see an eight-hour day as a breeze. My clients were happy, they were getting great results, and I felt like I had truly arrived. Getting my business working for me instead of the other way around opened my eyes to the importance of doing what feels right for me.

Around this time, I attended a business development workshop hosted by a friend where the speaker delivered a fantastic lecture on feminine business success and the challenges of being a woman running a business. She addressed the expectations placed on women and the burdens we shoulder while trying to succeed. It was a profound talk.

As I sat there, it felt like the clouds parted, and suddenly, I received what I call a "download," an insight about a specific target revenue I should aim for. The number seemed impossible to me. The guidance I received was to go home and get all my financial records up to date.

I had been feeling so overwhelmed and convinced that I was going to fail that I hadn't been keeping up with my billing or accounting. This only reinforced the imposter syndrome I was experiencing. I felt like I would never succeed, that my life wasn't truly my own, and that this whole situation wasn't real.

When I went home and finally did my books, I realized I was already hitting the financial targets that came through during that presentation. While my work was never about financial goals, it was astonishing for me to see that I was achieving numbers that had previously seemed impossible. Later, I learned that the woman sitting next to me at the event was a Reiki master, a practitioner of an energy-based healing modality that supports shifts in underlying patterns and the body's capacity to restore balance. I felt a shift—her presence seemed to clear energetic interference tied to shame I didn't even know I was carrying: shame for wanting more, for following my passion, and for dreaming big.

I thought I was avoiding my books because they would prove I was a failure. But the truth was even more unsettling: I was avoiding them because they would prove I was a success, a success I didn't believe I could be.

That experience showed me how shame can obscure clarity and block alignment. It reinforced what had already been becoming clear to me: when I stopped avoiding the obstacle and faced it directly, the path forward revealed itself.

Through my subsequent research on developing and strengthening business intuition, I discovered that Reiki can be incredibly helpful in that process.[1,2] I even became a Reiki master, largely because of what I had learned. Before I started studying, I didn't really believe in Reiki, and here I was, seeing its impact.

I always knew how to be the version of myself that faced failure. I knew how to be the person who worked hard and struggled, but I didn't know how to embody the version of

---

1. Shatliff, B. (2025, March 5). Reiki for entrepreneurs and the role of energy healing in success. *Brainz*. https://www.brainzmagazine.com/post/reiki-for-entrepreneurs-and-the-role-of-energy-healing-in-success

2. Harris, M. (2017, January 26). What the medical intuitive to the world's elite can teach any entrepreneur feeling stuck. *Forbes*. https://www.forbes.com/sites/meggentaylor/2017/01/26/what-the-medical-intuitive-to-the-worlds-elite-can-teach-any-entrepreneur-feeling-stuck/

myself that could succeed. For the first time in my life, I had to confront that successful version of myself.

To facilitate this change, I hired a business coach. Initially, I sought her guidance for leadership development, as I was working in a large international community and wanted to enhance my leadership skills for different cultures and backgrounds. However, our sessions quickly shifted focus to straightforward business development: defining my vision, mission, and making basic business decisions.

Through that process, I was introduced to a philosophy that would later become foundational to my own work as a coach: the idea that clients are naturally creative, resourceful, and whole. Coaching wasn't about fixing what was broken. Instead, it invited me to look forward and discover what was already present but perhaps not yet fully trusted. It was my first real experience with the forward-focused dimension of coaching, where the work is not to prove worthiness but to recognize that it already exists.

Every time I brought a new idea or question to my coach, her suggestions aligned perfectly with what I had either already done or was considering. Everything pointed to one central theme that I reminded myself regularly: You have a good head for business, Shelley. You have solid instincts. You have a natural ability to recognize what works for you, and you excel at following those instincts and seeing things through.

In 2012, for the first time in my life, all the artifice and complicated storylines fell away. As my business started to unwind and multiply, I unpacked early childhood conditioning and life experiences that had shaped me. I later discovered influences from my ancestors as well.

I had been manifesting all along—putting out wishes and watching for things to show up so I could then follow. There were always a few hiccups; the wishes weren't always aligned with what I truly wanted for my life. Once I assembled my energetic board of advisors to help me examine all the filters and beliefs I had taken for granted, such as "This is just the way things are" or "This is who I am," I began to see those notions not as absolutes but as *filters*.

This process illuminated the blind spots I had been unaware of. It disrupted patterns I'd grown accustomed to, assumptions about the way things were. I confronted limiting beliefs head-on. "I'll never succeed" became "I *am* successful, and I will continue to be.

"I'm not good enough with finances" became "I'm already making good money with my business and on track for significant growth."

Standing on my own two feet in this new reality, I encountered the version of myself that succeeds. As I stood there, everything I believed about my life story began to turn upside down. I reexamined all my relationships, misaligned business ventures, and past narratives, viewing them through a new lens and opening up a world of possibilities for the future.

And this was only the beginning.

Releasing Toxic Shame

Toxic shame is not simply the belief that one made a mistake. It is a deep, identity-level conviction of being fundamentally flawed or unworthy.[3] Psychologist Silvan Tomkins described it as a pathological form of shame that becomes a core wound, shaping how we see ourselves.[4]

From an energy psychology perspective, shame lodges in the energetic field, particularly in the solar plexus chakra, Manipura, the center of personal power and will.[5] Modern psychology supports this understanding. Shame is not only cognitive. It is somatic. It is stored in the nervous system and the gut, and embodied, trauma-informed practices can help it release.

In chakra systems, the solar plexus is associated with self-esteem, autonomy, and inner authority. When this center is healthy, it fuels clarity, boundaries, and purposeful action. When toxic shame takes root, that energy becomes constricted. It often reflects internalized messages such as "Don't take up space," "Don't ask for help," and "You should be able to do this alone." Toxic shame dims leadership at its source.

---

3. Tangney, J. P., & Dearing, R. L. (2002). *Shame and guilt*. New York, NY: Guilford Press.

4. Tomkins, S. S. (1963). *Affect imagery consciousness: Vol. II. the negative affects*. New York: Springer.

5. Judith, A. (2004). *Eastern body, western mind: Psychology and the chakra system as a path to the self*. Celestial Arts of Ten Speed Press.

The celiac plexus, located in this region, connects to the vagus nerve and the digestive system, both highly sensitive to emotional stress. Imaging studies show that shame activates this area, linking psychological trauma to gut-based dysregulation.

For conscious entrepreneurs and high performers, this shutdown can appear as chronic self-doubt, perfectionism or imposter syndrome, overgiving or boundary collapse, fear of visibility, indecision or powerlessness, digestive issues, or fatigue. Shame alters how we process and perceive the world. As Stephen Porges, the founder of the polyvagal theory, explains, the nervous system must assess safety before shifting from defense to connection.[6] Shame keeps the system in threat mode.

Research shows that toxic shame cannot be healed through mindset work alone. It requires safe, embodied witnessing and co-regulation. Being seen in wholeness, even in struggle, helps dissolve shame.

You need not prove your worth. You already are it.

When shame drives performance, performance becomes performative. Work becomes a display of worthiness rather than an expression of truth.

Clearing shame from the solar plexus restores inner authority. The shift is subtle but profound. It moves from proving to trusting, from perfection to wholeness, and from external validation to internal alignment.

This is a new model of peak performance, one in which intuition is clear and work reflects who we are. It begins with dismantling toxic shame, one breath, one boundary, one brave truth at a time.

Tara Swart on Neuroscience for Business: Why Organizations Behave Like the Brain

Tara Swart draws a compelling parallel between the human brain and the businesses we run: both are complex, adaptive systems that thrive on coherence, clarity, and well-regulated flow. Her central premise is that business challenges are often reflections

---

6. Porges, S. W. (2011). *The polyvagal theory: Neurophysiological foundations of emotions, attachment, communication, and self-regulation*. New York, NY: W. W. Norton & Company.

of underlying neurological patterns. When leaders understand how the brain processes information, allocates energy, or responds to uncertainty, they can build organizations that are more resilient, innovative, and aligned.[7]

Swart argues that businesses function like neural networks. They operate through interconnected relationships, feedback loops, communication pathways, and competing priorities—much like synapses firing across different brain regions.[8] When communication is clear and resources are well-distributed, both brains and businesses perform at a higher level. When the system is overloaded, unclear, or chronically stressed, both experience breakdowns in decision-making, creativity, and long-term planning.[9]

A key idea she emphasizes is the need for cognitive flexibility—the brain's capacity to switch perspectives, learn new strategies, and tolerate uncertainty. In the business context, cognitive flexibility becomes organizational agility. Companies that cannot adapt to shifting markets mirror brains locked in rigid neural firing patterns. Conversely, high-performing organizations mirror brains with strong prefrontal–limbic integration: grounded, reflective, emotionally balanced, and capable of strategic foresight.[10]

Swart also highlights the importance of psychological safety, which she frames through the lens of neurobiology. When the brain perceives a threat, the amygdala restricts access to the prefrontal cortex, impairing creativity, empathy, and long-term planning. Businesses plagued by fear-based cultures replicate this neural shutdown. Leaders who cultivate trust and emotional regulation foster environments where people can innovate,

---

7. Swart, T., Chisholm, K., & Brown, P. (2015). *Neuroscience for leadership: Harnessing the brain gain advantage.* London: Palgrave Macmillan.

8. Holland, J. H. (2006). Studying complex adaptive systems. *Journal of Systems Science and Complexity, 19*(1), 1–8.

9. Boyatzis, R. E., Rochford, K., & Taylor, S. N. (2015). *The role of the positive emotional attractor in vision and shared vision: Toward effective leadership, relationships, and engagement.* Frontiers in Psychology, 6, 670.

10. Rock, D., & Schwartz, J. (2006). The neuroscience of leadership. *Strategy + Business, 43,* 1–10.

collaborate, and take intelligent risks—conditions similar to what the brain requires to learn and reorganize itself through neuroplasticity.[11,12]

Another parallel Swart draws is the concept of energy management. The brain has finite glucose, oxygen, and attentional resources. Businesses face similar constraints: time, budget, bandwidth, and cognitive load. When a leader tries to operate on willpower alone or a company stretches itself thin, both systems default to short-term survival modes. Purpose, rest, strategic focus, and emotional regulation are not luxuries—they are the foundations of peak performance.

Her model also reinforces why emotionally intelligent leadership is not soft skills work but neurological infrastructure. Self-awareness, empathy, and emotional regulation activate the social engagement networks associated with the brain's ability to connect, collaborate, and solve complex problems. These interpersonal capacities become collective capacities, shaping the entire business ecosystem.[13]

From a manifestation and alchemy perspective, Swart's neuroscience translates directly to business as a living energy system. A coherent internal map—whether neural or organizational—creates the conditions for clarity, synchronicity, and aligned action. Dysfunction in either realm reflects noise in the system, competing agendas, or unintegrated fear responses.

Core Principles from Swart's Model

- Businesses behave like brains. Both are systems made of interconnected nodes requiring clear communication, structure, and regulated flow.
- Stress impairs strategic functioning. Threat states reduce innovation, collaboration, and long-term vision.

11. Edmondson, A. (1999). Psychological safety and learning behavior in work teams. *Administrative Science Quarterly, 44*(2), 350–383.

12. Immordino-Yang, M. H., Darling-Hammond, L., & Krone, C. R. (2019). *The brain basis for integrated social, emotional, and academic development.* Aspen Institute.

13. Senge, P. M. (2006). *The fifth discipline: The art and practice of the learning organization.* New York, NY: Doubleday.

- Cognitive flexibility equals business adaptability. The ability to shift perspectives is essential for growth.
- Energy and attention are limited resources. Focus must be intentionally allocated to high-value tasks.
- Emotionally intelligent leadership creates high-performance cultures. Trust, empathy, and psychological safety unlock the organization's collective intelligence.
- Neuroplasticity maps to organizational evolution. Just as the brain rewires through repetition and intention, businesses transform through consistent behavior, clarity of purpose, and aligned action.

In essence, Swart positions neuroscience as a blueprint for conscious, adaptive leadership—one that echoes the framework of treating the business as an energetic field that responds to clarity, intention, coherence, and the capacity to regulate internal and external stressors.

Chapter Five

Thriving From Enough

Things were finally working out for me. The manifesting process had begun from a place of believing I was enough. For years, I had worked toward that realization, but living from it was something entirely different. When the belief that I was enough finally took root, it didn't just change how I felt about myself. It changed how I showed up in my life, my work, and my business.

With time, my doubts faded away, and that self-acceptance gave way to genuine confidence. Instead of holding myself back or confining my potential, I expanded. This expansion felt exhilarating—like anything was possible. But it was also unfamiliar territory. For most of my life, my identity was organized around effort, striving, and proving myself. Now I was learning how to live inside a version of my life where things were actually working.

My business was thriving. I was fully booked, and my clients were achieving great results. As my reputation spread, I found I had time to rest. For the first time in a while, I was going home at a reasonable hour, getting enough sleep, eating well, socializing, practicing yoga, and truly enjoying New York City on a deeper level than I had in years. I felt fantastic, looked great, and others noticed. People asked me how I did it.

What I didn't yet realize was that success brings its own kind of initiation. Expansion reveals the parts of ourselves that still expect things to fall apart. As my work grew and my visibility increased, deeper patterns began to surface—old habits of overworking, inherited beliefs about success, and the uncomfortable realization that stepping into leadership meant becoming someone I had never allowed myself to be before.

Success wasn't the challenge anymore. Learning how to live inside it was.

As I was revisiting Caroline Myss, I listened to her audio course called "Advanced Chakra Anatomy." I found it to be incredibly similar to the process outlined in Keith Harrell's book, *Attitude is Everything*.[1] To recap, the main idea is that if you truly believe in where you want to be, no amount of time is too long, and there's nothing that would indicate it's never going to work out. If you are completely committed, it will always work out. You just need to map out your path. Harrell provides inspiring case studies of people who knew where they wanted to be, and sometimes it took them 20 years to get there. It's all about having an unwavering belief in your success and letting go of the notion that if something doesn't happen right away, it will never happen.

In "Advanced Chakra Anatomy," Myss introduces an understanding of subtle energy anatomy, explaining that inspiration comes in through the crown of your head and must flow through each of your body's chakras: from the seventh to the first. This journey from inspiration to manifestation follows cycles, and, as in her case studies, it can take people 20, 30, or even 50 years for their goals to materialize. She emphasizes that these experiences are part of your spiritual destiny and purpose; they are not random.

Her audio course resonated deeply. I had experienced similar synchronicities and small signs on my own journey. I did wonder if there's a way to make this process happen more quickly. Could it be possible to accelerate one's journey? I reflected on how I could bring to life what was awakening within me, not just for my benefit, but for the world's benefit as well.

During a few months of introspection, I downloaded a wealth of information and inspiration about how my awakening could inform decision-making during times of uncertainty. I realized that my business could be the platform where my gifts come alive in ways that people truly need. It's about finding that intersection between what people are searching for and what I have to offer. I didn't want my work to be merely transactional; I wanted it to be relational.

I was gathering a lot of information and writing extensively, almost channeling the information. I learned later that what I was doing is called "automatic writing," a

1. Harrell, K. (2003). *Attitude is everything: 10 Life-Changing Steps to Turning Attitude Into Action*. HarperBusiness.

practice originating in late-19th-century spiritualism in which a person writes in a relaxed, non-analytical state to access subconscious or intuitive insight.[2] This process marked the beginning of the creative and intuitive work that has been unfolding ever since, laying the foundation for how I tap into deeper insight and make sense of the material that informs my practice.

During this exploration, I had an experience I would describe as "remembering the future." I could see and know things before they happened, but it wasn't in the traditional psychic sense that we might imagine.

Instead, it felt more about potentialities and possible timelines. By recalling these future possibilities and connecting with the feeling of having already achieved them, I discovered I could align myself with them and start bringing them into reality. I was taking a course by a woman named Cyndi Dale, who specializes in chakra anatomy and has written extensively about energy anatomy and subtle energy.

In this course, she discussed how the function of chakras can vary based on lineage and ancestry. She mentioned that the Cherokee use their chakras to access future timelines. With Cherokee ancestry in my family line, I wondered, *Is that what's happening to me?* I felt compelled to understand this more deeply, so I booked a consultation with her.

During our session, she validated my intuition and connection, saying, "It's more than something inherited through your ancestry, Shelley. The work you're bringing in will help people achieve their dreams more effortlessly, not by bypassing the challenges. They often believe they must climb a mountain, but you're here to show them that they can simply go around it."

Her words were profound. She told me that I wasn't necessarily meant to study these lineages and practices but rather to translate what was being carried through me into a more contemporary language. This resonated deeply with what I had been channeling and receiving.

---

2. Cardeña, E., Lindström, L., Goldin, P., Van Westen, D., & Mårtensson, J. (2023). A neurophenomenological fMRI study of a spontaneous automatic writer and a hypnotic cohort. *Brain and Cognition, 170*, 106060. https://doi.org/10.1016/j.bandc.2023.106060.

I began working with this concept more fully, both for myself and my clients. I envisioned where I wanted to be, placed myself in that future timeline, and started to work backward. This approach shaped my daily practice.

In coaching, we often discuss SMART goals: Specific, Measurable, Actionable, Realistic, and Time-bound. I chose to refer to goals as "alchemy items" instead. Rather than mentally pondering how to bridge the gap from where I am to where I want to be, I envisioned myself in that desired future and created SMART goals by working backward from there.

What actions did I need to take to transform my current reality into what I envisioned? The approach was trusting that something even better than I alone could imagine might emerge—rather than trying to hack that specific outcome. Through this journey of unpacking and unwinding, I gained a deeper understanding that many of our life experiences, impressions, and habits are stored as patterned imprints within us, like records. This process helps to accelerate the release of old information and filters, freeing up energy for what you want to create.[3]

I remember visiting my old studio and being met with expressions of shock when people saw me. "Wow! What are you doing? You look amazing!" they exclaimed. Eventually, people started asking for my help, which inspired me to offer immersive programs sharing my method. I began with small offerings, a few weekly and monthly programs, and gradually, my business grew. My work transformed beyond a nine-to-five job to a realm where I was creating and running online programs, teaching courses on weekends, and connecting with an international community. I felt like I was on fire. I was thrilled to help others and ecstatic that they noticed the positive changes in me. At the time, I was enjoying every moment of it. However, I found myself slipping back into overworking and overextending.

Then, I received a call from an old colleague. She was trying to persuade me to come work for her, and she also wanted help with her business struggles. I was in such an expanded mindset that going back to working for someone else didn't seem like an option. I loved

---

3. Wood, W., & Rünger, D. (2016). Psychology of habit. *Annual Review of Psychology, 67*, 289–314. https://doi.org/10.1146/annurev-psych-122414-033417

and admired her and genuinely wanted to help, so I said, "No, I can't come work for you, but I would love to coach you."

I guided her through a process similar to my own business journey but tailored to her specific interests and goals. We uncovered an issue in her business that she was reluctant to confront. She feared that facing it would reveal something unpleasant, that she was a failure or not good enough. This was akin to my own hesitance to look at my numbers or do my accounting, as I worried it would expose my shortcomings.

Together, we worked to navigate her fears and examined the aspects of her business she had avoided, including the necessary crunching of numbers. She had two storefront businesses in New York City. One was doing well, while the other was struggling. She also had an opportunity to open a business on the West Coast, but she couldn't imagine managing that while dealing with the challenges of her existing struggling business in New York City.

Throughout this entire process, she received her lease renewal. By crunching the numbers and evaluating what it would truly take for her to thrive in the second New York location, she realized that with the proposed rent increase, it was no longer viable for her to keep both storefronts open. However, because we had done some energy work and focused on business energetics, something interesting happened. The schedules of her clients and staff seamlessly integrated with those of her other location. As a result, she was able to merge the two businesses into one location, transforming her previously successful business into an even more thriving one.

What initially felt like a failure turned into a remarkable success. Not only did she successfully merge the businesses into a more prosperous location in New York City, but it also freed up her time and resources to pursue the West Coast opportunity. This expansion allowed her to establish a national presence, with locations on both the East Coast and the West Coast. The outcome was nothing short of incredible.

I initially started this journey thinking I wasn't good at business, but I began to realize that perhaps this was a valuable service I could offer. More and more people sought out my help. It dawned on me that I might be better at coaching others in business than coaching them as individuals.

When I help one person, I positively impact their life. But when I work with a business, I am helping the owner and the staff and the community that the business serves. Guiding a practitioner to improve their business creates a ripple effect far beyond what I could achieve on my own.

As this understanding grew, so did the excitement. I started hosting global events focused on business energetics for healers. I not only organized continuing education courses but also large non-profit fundraisers. These events attracted practitioners from around the world to discuss business energetics.

I was on fire with enthusiasm, but I also found myself losing steam. As all these events unfolded, I felt stretched thin, and there was a nagging sense that something beneath the surface remained unresolved. Everything in my life seemed to be going well, beyond my wildest dreams, yet there was still a heaviness I couldn't shake. About a year after fully launching my practice, I attended a practitioner intensive where I had the opportunity to receive guidance from a master healer. My main request was simple: I wanted to feel more positive about my life.

During the session, he identified ancestral patterns that I had inherited, patterns that were influencing me in ways I hadn't considered before. This was the first time anyone had approached ancestral influence in terms of inherited patterns that could interfere with how I was experiencing my life, and it was a game-changer for me. At the same time, I found myself wondering, *What do I do with this information? What does it actually mean for my life?*

At one point in the session, he used a phrase that immediately caught my attention: **psychic inversion**. He described it as a kind of energetic reversal, where the subtle energy system becomes, in his words, almost "inside out." Rather than orienting naturally toward growth and stability, the nervous system begins organizing itself around vigilance—constantly listening for safety. In that state, the psyche can unintentionally push away the very things it desires while reinforcing the patterns that keep it stuck.

He also pointed out how this pattern might be affecting my life directly. Opportunities could arrive, but they didn't seem to stay because there was instability in my capacity to hold onto what was working—as if some deeper layer of my system expected things to fall apart.

As I reflected on the session afterward, I saw how closely this description mirrored the pattern I had been experiencing in both my business and my personal life. On the surface, everything was expanding, yet some deeper part of me still braced for loss.

When something shifted during the session, it felt as though a pressure valve was released. The heaviness that had been lingering beneath the surface lifted, and the plateau I had been experiencing in my business suddenly started moving again. Bookings increased, opportunities opened, and the sense of stagnation that had been quietly sitting underneath everything dissolved.

At the time, I didn't fully understand what had happened. But the experience stayed with me. I kept returning to the idea of inversion and wondering how these subtle energetic patterns might shape perception, behavior, and even our ability to receive success.

Later that year, I traveled to a conference in Malta, where I was recognized for my role in building a global practitioner community. I had envisioned an environment where everyone would share my excitement and inspiration for expansion. While that vision did come to fruition, I also encountered a secondary wave of individuals who seemed to be looking to take advantage of my newfound visibility. Someone invited me to an event where a famous medium channeled messages from those who have passed in a room full of people who paid a lot to be there. My colleague turned to me and said, "Mediumship is the new rock 'n' roll. You should get an agent and be famous!" I was terrified at what I saw. Something sacred was being exploited ... for what gain other than fame or money?

I was taken aback by the darker side of recognition, perhaps a bit naïve in my belief that everyone has good intentions. Some of the people and organizations I worked with believed in mutual support and growth, but others had opportunistic motives, which let an energy of sabotage creep into my efforts. As a result, the momentum I had built waned, and my achievements slowed down.

I was exhausted and processing more than ever what it means to be a healer. In the midst of all this, I was invited to be featured in a photojournalistic article about the healers of New York. While the shoot was physically and mentally demanding, I loved the recognition and visibility the feature gave to healing, which is an important part of our culture, even in a place as metropolitan as New York. I was conflicted, navigating the tension between being seen as a "healer celebrity" and being a true healer.

In the end, I chose the path that mattered to me: showing up in a way that creates real, meaningful shifts for people. I wasn't interested in recognition or superficial visibility—I wanted the work itself to be the source of impact. This led me to decline opportunities that didn't feel aligned so I could stay focused on the work itself.

In December 2013, my client, Anjali—a well-known model living in India who had been coming to New York for years—decided to stay and work with me full-time after developing a health issue she feared would escalate without deeper support. We entered an intensive six-to-eight-week period of work together, and thankfully, she did heal.

When it came time for Anjali to return to India, she told me she was afraid to go back alone. She worried that the illness would return if I weren't there to help her integrate the changes. So she asked if I would travel back with her.

In a matter of days, I secured a visa—something nearly impossible to do on short notice—and arranged to stay in India for a month. The plan was simple: an apartment in Mumbai, a few hours of work with her each week, and the rest of the time left open to travel and work on personal projects.

But when I arrived, the apartment was—you guessed it—still under construction. Jayant, our host and my client's partner, had recently experienced a major business collapse. He had gone from running a large architectural firm with hundreds of employees to managing only a few interns. Nothing about the situation was stable. The original plan dissolved immediately, and I ended up traveling with them throughout India for the entire month.

There were extraordinary moments. I remember being on a speedboat from Mumbai to Alibaug, transporting a Pilates reformer across the water, then driving it through rural roads to reach Jayant's stunning property. There were dinner parties hosted in my honor, attended by well-known figures in Indian society and visiting dignitaries. The experience was surreal—and yet, my focus had to stay grounded in the purpose of the trip: Anjali's healing and her integration back into her life.

It was one of the most challenging months of my life. The environment was chaotic and emotionally charged, and I had to hold exceptionally strong boundaries. Anjali and Jayant had grand ideas for me—opening a healing center in India, moving there, becoming part of their circle. It all sounded beautiful, but it wasn't the purpose of my being there. My responsibility was Anjali's healing, not the distractions around us.

Amid all of this, there was another layer unfolding behind the scenes.

Jayant avoided working with me at all costs. He was generous, entertaining, and attentive, but emotionally evasive. The dynamic between us carried tension and miscommunication, as if my presence was somehow ungrateful or intrusive. But beneath the surface, I could feel that something else was moving within him. Something old, unprocessed, and asking for resolution. So I centered myself, practiced self-care, and held space for whatever was trying to surface.

On the last night of the trip, everything shifted. He asked for a session. What emerged was profound.

His system was carrying a lifetime of unresolved grief—the deaths of important people during his childhood, more losses in adulthood, and a long pattern of "moving on" from his pain without ever fully grieving. All of it had begun to surface as his life unraveled around him: a previous divorce that was culturally stigmatized, the collapse of a once-thriving business, and the emergence of a new, unconventional romance with Anjali, a woman working in Western fashion, that challenged both tradition and identity.

But there was also something remarkable in Jayant—an innovative, ecological approach to architecture that broke from the dominant model of modern construction. Where the industry was moving toward monolithic structures that separated humans from their environment, he was pioneering integrative designs that brought people into harmony with their natural surroundings. It mirrored his own psychic inversion: an inner split between the old structures falling apart and the new, more holistic vision trying to emerge.

As our session concluded, he looked at me with clarity and said, "I get it. I need to finally grieve. I need to heal."

At that moment, the entire trip made sense. The chaos, the resistance, the detours—it had all been leading to the unraveling of something deeper than the logistical challenges of a failed apartment or a collapsed business. The trip wasn't only about Anjali's healing. It was also about Jayant's. And in supporting both processes, I was fulfilling the role I was meant to play there—one that wasn't planned but revealed. Only then was I able to leave, knowing the work had completed itself in the way it was always meant to.

Even as I expanded and embraced the version of myself that could succeed, I was still carrying old patterns with me. After that fateful trip, I started to recognize that some of these patterns might be rooted in my early childhood conditioning, family of origin, and ancestry. My family didn't even acknowledge my trip had happened—they were upset that I said yes to Anjali instead of coming home for Christmas. Finding success in new ways challenged the family narrative that I was "irresponsible" because I "didn't toe the family line."

I was dedicating my time and energy to the vision of making the world a better place and creating positive change. Throughout this journey, I continued to experience things that kept me grounded in my values. As I became more rooted in these values, I observed my habits evolving and deepening into something different.

I was trying to navigate the space where something greater than I had imagined was unfolding for me. I set the intention to make an impact on the world, and I consistently manifested experiences that helped me envision a bigger future. Importantly, I learned how to navigate this journey without burning out, avoiding the martyr mentality, and refraining from sacrificing my own needs for the greater good. This process taught me that the success of my business was tied to me being my best self.

I was learning how to energetically partner with my business. When my business thrived, it supported me. Each experience contributed to my growth, allowing me to excel at my strengths and embody them in a more sustainable way. It felt as if my business were guiding me toward encounters that would challenge me and help me grow.

This journey continually reminded me that I was already enough. With that realization came the freedom to release constant striving and to let go of outdated beliefs that no longer aligned with the vision I was creating. Setting an intention and imagining what I hoped to build did not always lead to the outcomes I expected, but it often led to something better.

Over time, this approach became a framework through which I could experience both business and life more fully. Business and life began to feel less like a race toward a destination and more like an unfolding process filled with meaningful experiences along the way. From 2012 to 2015, I learned to pull back and let my business shape me into someone who could thrive within it.

Remember, while you may have an idea of where you want to be, the map is not the territory. Living authentically means that each unfolding moment leads you toward outcomes that help you sustain the version of yourself that was once difficult to embody. Now, you're living that reality every day.

During this time, I developed habits and strategies that made it easier to inhabit that future state. I also integrated a daily practice where I grounded myself in the intention of what I wanted to create and then asked myself how I was doing in that regard. I would focus on the first three things that came to mind. Through this process, I completely transformed my relationship with goals. I let go of the idea of who I wanted to be and allowed my business to support me in realizing my true self through experience and the opportunities that were unfolding around me. I revisited Caroline Myss's archetypes of survival, which are rooted in how we compromise our true values and beliefs in order to feel safe in the world. I had been living from these archetypes—for far too long.

Myss referred to them as "shadow selves," the parts of ourselves that we ignore or deny. However, I recognized that these weren't just shadows for me; they were how I identified myself. I needed to uncover a "positive shadow"—the part of us that holds our unrealized gifts and the strengths and leadership capacities we have buried to maintain a sense of belonging or safety. It was time for me to get to know the part of myself that had been hiding: my successful self.

So, I began working with the positive shadow archetypes of the Intuitive Alchemist, the Investigator, the Entrepreneur, and the Champion. I started integrating that energy into my daily practice. I asked myself, *Who do I need to embody today? My Entrepreneur or my Champion?* This practice taught me how to live in a state of success, not as a distant idea or an unattainable goal, but as a grounded reality that I could experience on a day-to-day basis. I had spent years striving to be enough. Now I was practicing remembering that I already was.

Positive Shadow

In psychological terms, what I call the "positive shadow" refers to the strengths and capacities that individuals under-identify with because they conflict with their established self-concept. Carl Jung originally described the shadow as containing disowned aspects of the self within the broader framework of archetypal psychology.[4] Although Jung's early work focused primarily on socially undesirable traits such as aggression, envy, or resentment, later interpretations of analytic psychology acknowledge that the shadow can also contain positive qualities that remain unclaimed because they challenge a person's existing identity structure.

Self-discrepancy theory proposes that tension arises when there is a gap between one's actual self and ideal or possible selves.[5] In some cases, individuals defensively minimize strengths that feel inconsistent with their established narrative. Abraham Maslow referred to this phenomenon as the "Jonah Complex," describing the tendency to fear one's own highest potential or greatness.[6] This pattern also aligns with Robert Kegan and Lisa Lahey's concept of "immunity to change," which proposes that individuals unconsciously resist growth when new capacities threaten existing identity structures or psychological equilibrium.[7]

Research in positive psychology further supports the importance of identifying and applying character strengths. The VIA Classification identifies 24 universal strengths associated with well-being and performance.[8]. Gallup's CliftonStrengths research similarly demonstrates that individuals who intentionally apply their strengths experience higher productivity and workplace engagement.[9] Strength use is positively associated with engagement, life satisfaction, and resilience and may be underused as well as

---

4. Jung, C. G. (1959). *Aion: Researches into the phenomenology of the self.* Princeton University Press.

5. Higgins, E. T. (1987). Self-discrepancy: A theory relating self and affect. *Psychological Review, 94*(3), 319–340. Markus, H., & Nurius, P. (1986). Possible selves. *American Psychologist, 41*(9), 954–969.

6. Maslow, A. H. (1971). *The farther reaches of human nature.* Viking Press.

7. Kegan, R., & Lahey, L. L. (2009). *Immunity to change: How to overcome it and unlock potential in yourself and your organization.* Harvard Business Press.

8. Peterson, C., & Seligman, M. E. P. (2004). *Character strengths and virtues: A handbook and classification.* Oxford University Press.

9. Rath, T. (2007). *StrengthsFinder 2.0.* Gallup Press.

overused, suggesting that avoidance of one's strongest capacities can quietly limit effectiveness.[10]

In coaching contexts, this often appears as over-identification with protective patterns such as procrastination, perfectionism, or self-sabotage, while under-identifying with leadership, creativity, or influence capacities that are equally present. Intentional Change Theory emphasizes the importance of articulating and emotionally connecting with an ideal self-vision to facilitate sustainable development.[11] Reframing protective patterns as underdeveloped strengths aligns with this strengths-based developmental approach.

This shift is further supported by research on curiosity and optimism. Curiosity enhances learning, adaptability, and psychological flexibility,[12] while optimism is associated with greater goal persistence, resilience, and recovery from stress.[13] When individuals reinterpret self-protective behaviors as signals of unrealized strengths, they move from a deficit framework toward a growth-oriented identity.

Positive shadow work invites us to reclaim the confidence, creativity, and power we've buried—and step into the leader we're meant to be.

What if the part of yourself you've feared wasn't your weakness but your strength?

When most people think of the shadow, they imagine anger, jealousy, or shame. But the shadow also contains what is too radiant or powerful for us to accept. This is the positive shadow: the creativity or brilliance we exile because it doesn't match our self-story.

This work becomes especially important when we over-identify with the part of us that sabotages or assumes things never work out.

---

10. Niemiec, R. M. (2018). *Character strengths interventions: A field guide for practitioners.* Hogrefe Publishing.

11. Boyatzis, R. E. (2006). An overview of intentional change from a complexity perspective. Journal of Management Development, 25(7), 607–623.

12. Kashdan, T. B., Rose, P., & Fincham, F. D. (2004). Curiosity and exploration: Facilitating positive subjective experiences and personal growth. Journal of Personality Assessment, 82(3), 291–305.

13. Carver, C. S., & Scheier, M. F. (2002). Optimism. In C. R. Snyder & S. J. Lopez (Eds.), Handbook of positive psychology (pp. 231–243). Oxford University Press.

Carl Jung described archetypes as universal energies within the collective unconscious that shape how we think and act. Caroline Myss later defined four core archetypes connected to survival. I use this archetypal language as a developmental tool to help leaders balance shadow tendencies with untapped gifts.

Caroline Myss's survival archetypes illustrate this clearly:

The Victim feels powerless. Its hidden gift is the Champion, who overcomes challenges.The Child appears as fear or dependency. Within it lies the Intuitive Alchemist, who transforms through creativity and wonder.The Prostitute compromises dreams for safety. Beneath it is the Entrepreneur, who takes aligned risks.The Saboteur shows up as procrastination or perfectionism. Its higher expression is the Investigator, who channels disruption into curiosity.

Each of these archetypes represents a transformation—from feeling stuck to asking, How is what's happening part of things working out for me? That question invites curiosity and optimism, qualities shown to strengthen resilience, improve learning, and support a constructive relationship with change.

When we see shadow in this way, we stop viewing it as "bad" and start recognizing it as a gateway to our unlived gifts.

Chapter Six

Business as Teacher

After my first year at the integrative practice, following a period of healing experiences, travel, and personal growth, I was presented with an opportunity to expand my work. At the time, I believed I was simply taking the next step in my business, but in hindsight, that period would become one of the most important teachers of my life. I entered into a partnership agreement with a large wellness center and opened my own office, hosting clients and events in a historic landmark building between Times Square and Grand Central Station. The rent was significant, but the location felt like an important step forward.

I remained there for two and a half years, yet a familiar pattern emerged: business would begin to pick up, then fall off again. Although I joined as a partner, I operated more like a tenant. This dynamic was not new for me. Several of my business relationships had begun with the promise of partnership but gradually placed me in a supporting role.

I entered this arrangement hoping it would be different. I imagined a space where I could host courses and events while collaborating with someone who shared my values and vision. Over time, however, it became difficult to launch initiatives. Events were often canceled at the last minute, and although I invited my business partner, Margaret, to attend and explore referral possibilities, it became clear that our collaboration was limited.

However, the challenges in this experience pushed me to deepen my approach to working with my business as its own energy system, leading me to develop new tools and ways of engaging with it.

Driven by my vision of making a global impact through fundraising and connection events, I faced consistent challenges. I loved the work and the community I was building, but I was doing everything myself, and something would inevitably slip through the cracks. At the same time, a parallel pattern emerged: whenever I encountered a challenge, the resources I needed would arrive. Managing the rent and operating at a higher budget level than ever before pushed me to learn how to support a business at that scale.

In many ways, it was a positive kind of stress. I was acclimating to the role of a high-performance business owner, and my business seemed to be revealing blind spots—where I was overexerting myself and where I could focus more strategically for better outcomes. It was a deep period of learning, yet I often felt inadequate.

Despite the growth in my business, I struggled with imposter syndrome and took criticism personally. I wasn't defensive so much as uncertain. I felt as though everyone else understood what they were doing while I was flying blind, and I carried that mindset throughout my time in that space.

As my lease approached its end, Margaret and I discussed what renewal might look like. I wasn't sure I wanted to stay. I had learned a great deal, but I sensed it might be time for a different space—something with more ease and less force.

We eventually agreed on a month-to-month arrangement while I explored other options. Margaret found a new collaborator and began planning a coworking space for integrative health practitioners. It seemed like a perfect solution that would buy me time, and I felt as though my business was helping me find a new flow.

Within days, however, everything unraveled. I was sitting at the front desk when the new partner was leaving. I expressed my enthusiasm about working together and the future of the space. She looked startled, quickly left, and I never saw her again.

I soon learned that Margaret was struggling to maintain a sustainable business and that the coworking plan had already fallen apart. The realization completely reframed my experience in that space. For so long, I had assumed the difficulties were due to my own shortcomings, but it became clear that she, too, was under significant pressure in her business.

At that moment, I felt unexpectedly liberated.

Around the same time, I had been corresponding with someone interested in BizAttune coaching who happened to have office space in Greenwich Village near Union Square—an area of New York I loved. On a whim, I asked if she might be renting it. We had a wonderful conversation, and within a few days, I arranged to sell my office equipment and transition into her space, where everything I needed was already in place.

We planned to share the space: she would be there a few days a week, and I would be there two and a half days. I went from a hectic six- or seven-day-a-week practice to being in the office for only two and a half days and working from home the rest of the time. At first I was afraid I would fail—fear was a familiar pattern for me.

My body was clearly asking for a reset. Soon afterward, during meditation, I received a message from my business: *Do less. You're doing way too much.* The idea felt radical and unsettling, but I trusted it and began making changes.

Even so, my old patterns lingered. Part of me still believed that twelve-hour days, seven days a week, were the only way to succeed. My sense of purpose and the impact I wanted to make often justified neglecting my own health and needs.

Gradually, this guidance led me into a different rhythm. I experienced what felt like a flow state—a natural acceleration of everything I had been building. The BizAttune process helped me step out of my own way. It felt as if my business itself was guiding me toward greater ease.

To my surprise, the change worked. Clients loved the new space, and I started offering in-person sessions two and a half days a week while working the rest of the time remotely. I also launched an online program, Business Alchemy, to expand my reach.

A small group of dedicated clients joined to explore business energetics and develop business intuition. Although I had taught elements of this work before, this was the first time I committed to a year-long immersion with clients to observe how these tools worked in real time. Over the next three years, the results were tangible, both for my clients and for my own business.

As this unfolded, I recognized something important. In coaching and energy work, people often say that beliefs must change before success can occur. My experience suggested something different. When the conditions of life change—when the nervous system experiences greater safety and possibility—beliefs often shift naturally.

That insight became central to the BizAttune process. Instead of trying to force belief change, the work focuses on creating the circumstances in which old patterns can release on their own.

During this period, I experienced a new sense of freedom. I traveled to Costa Rica and participated in a month-long Prana Yoga training focused on the subtle energy body. The experience deepened my understanding of how ancient practices and modern neuroscience could inform my work.

When I first started my business, I saw it purely as a purpose-driven endeavor. I believed I had to choose between making a profit and making an impact. Over time, my business taught me that the two are not mutually exclusive. In fact, meaningful impact often requires a financially sustainable structure.

Taking time away from constant work allowed me to rest, deepen my practices, and expand my methods. It helped me return to my clients with greater clarity while continuing to develop the BizAttune process as a model for community, collaboration, and sustainable success.

As a business owner operating within a culture that assumes competition drives innovation, I have always felt a quiet resistance to competing. I entered the healing field believing it was rooted in collaboration, shared mission, and collective uplift. What surprised me was how competitive it could be—sometimes subtly, sometimes overtly—from a business and economic standpoint.

There were moments when I realized that leading with generosity and community spirit, without discernment, left me vulnerable to being undercut or overlooked. I had to mature quickly and learn that collaboration and boundaries are not opposites. Honoring my work required understanding market dynamics without becoming consumed by them.

At the same time, I recognized that I was highly competitive—but mostly with myself. I held myself to exacting standards and measured my growth against my own potential. That internal drive could be motivating, but it could also become harsh and tied too closely to success or failure.

The real shift came when I rooted my work more deeply in my values and long-term vision. That's when the reactive edge of competition dissolved, replaced by a constructive entrepreneurial drive grounded in innovation, integrity, and sustainable growth.

Instead of asking, "How do I win?" I asked, "How do I build something true?"

By no longer orienting my work around the competitive, performative edges of the wellness industry, I was able to carve out a path that felt structurally different.

The performative nature of wellness—where appearance can eclipse depth—often rewards amplifying people's perceived deficits. I didn't want to build a business around fixing people. I wanted to create work that engages the whole person.

That realization clarified my niche: alchemy and manifestation. In one application, desire became a form of self-study and personal growth. In another, those same principles translated into business—using intuition, energy, and conscious strategy to build something sustainable and alive.

When healing is framed primarily as problem-solving, it can become heavy and stress-inducing. Alchemy invites a different question: not "What's wrong?" but "What wants to emerge?"

This shift took pressure off both healing and success. Instead of obsessing over outcomes, clients focused on cultivating the conditions in which their gifts could take form. That intersection—where wellness informs entrepreneurship and entrepreneurship reinforces wellness—became the foundation of Business Alchemy.

I also leaned into community through small-group programs where members supported one another's growth rather than competing for visibility. The shift was not only strategic but philosophical: I stopped trying to win within someone else's framework and built within my own.

Even so, I often met people who appeared to be succeeding by every external metric yet still felt empty and unfulfilled.

During this period, I found myself with more free time to practice a technique known as the 30-day practice, designed to help rewire habits and foster healthy habits.[1,2] I had been practicing this for years as part of my initial efforts to develop intuition and business alchemy, and was able to dive even deeper into it.

When I went to Costa Rica for a month, I learned a tantric version of the 30-day practice that incorporated yoga nidra, essentially a form of self-hypnosis, along with a sankalpa, or intention. This technique involves hypnotizing oneself with a specific intention to reprogram the subconscious mind. It amazed me how similar the concepts were across different systems and teachings. As I expanded my practice, I moved from 30 days to 60 days, and eventually to 100 days, all while setting a strong intention and committing to this transformative process over time.

My life and business began transforming when I gave myself the time and freedom to engage in daily practice. This practice created an unwinding, allowing unconscious beliefs to surface. Unwinding, in this sense, meant recalibrating how my energy and attention were being used, shifting from sustaining an old version of myself to building a version capable of sustaining success.

I consciously set intentions for what I wanted to create and practiced embodying them. As I did, the patterns shaping my current experience emerged. I became aware of the unconscious beliefs influencing my thoughts and behaviors—many formed in early childhood and reinforced by culture. With that awareness, I could finally work with them rather than be driven by them.

I also became aware of the deep connection between intuition and being an empath. An empath is someone who is highly sensitive to subtle information, often processing a vast amount of it. As an empath, I tended to absorb others' thoughts, feelings, and emotions, often without realizing they weren't mine. It became overwhelming.

---

1. Gardner, B., Lally, P., & Wardle, J. (2012). *Making health habitual: the psychology of 'habit-formation' and general practice*. The British journal of general practice: the journal of the Royal College of General Practitioners, 62(605), 664–666. https://doi.org/10.3399/bjgp12X659466 .

2. Weiden, V. A. (2020, March). *How to form good habits? A longitudinal field study on the role of self-control in habit formation.* Frontiers. https://www.frontiersin.org/articles/10.3389/fpsyg.2020.00560/full

My internal messaging became cluttered with external influences, thoughts, and feelings that weren't necessarily my own. For instance, when I meditated and received insights into a business plan or strategy, I noticed that similar ideas would manifest among the friends I was spending time with. It felt as though I was picking up on their energy, and they were picking up on mine. I found myself questioning whether I had been influenced by their business plans or if they had drawn inspiration from mine.

Gradually, I learned to unpack these experiences and ground myself in different ways, allowing my intuition to align with my intentions. This process helped me organize my intuitive insights and make innovative decisions in the face of uncertainty. It also helped balance my nervous system, as both aspects supported each other simultaneously.

Over time, I became more confident in my abilities. As the BizAttune process yielded positive results and forward momentum, my excitement and investment in the practice grew.

In 2017, I made a pivotal decision: I fully embraced my business philosophy. I recognized that treating my business as a distinct energy system, complete with its own filters, was enhancing my insights, intuition, and ability to create beyond my previous limits. I was able to reduce the overwhelm of being an empath and of processing so much information in my body by offloading that burden onto my business. This perspective revealed possibilities I had never imagined before. I was all in; I wholeheartedly believed in this process and was ready to dream bigger than I ever had before.

To channel my intentions, I practiced the meditation I had been using to attune to what I was ready to create. Everything was flourishing—I was transforming people's lives through my work, and I owned a beautiful home and my dream property in upstate New York. I felt ready to expand even further.

During the meditation, I envisioned making a global impact. I embodied that vision fully, letting the feeling move through every part of my body. There was no doubt, only a deep sense that this future was possible.

I felt open, free, and expansive, filled with excitement for what lay ahead.

The next morning, I went to work and had a wonderful day with my clients. But when I returned home and checked the mail, I found a letter from the IRS stating that I owed $30,000 in taxes.

I froze. For a moment, I wondered if the entire vision I had felt so clearly the night before had just collapsed in a single piece of mail.

Just a day earlier, I had felt expansive and confident. Now shame and self-doubt flooded in. My mind immediately jumped to harsh conclusions: This must mean I'm not meant to succeed. How could I have been so irresponsible that I didn't even know about this debt?

Within minutes, I had gone from feeling radiant to feeling hollowed out, as though all the air had been pulled from my body. I climbed into bed and pulled the covers over my head.

Then I remembered something I had learned through my practice: the idea of the sacred circle. Once you initiate a process of growth and expansion, everything that arises becomes part of that unfolding.

If I had truly asked for expansion, perhaps this was the next step in the process.

The next day, I called my accountant to figure out what had happened. To our surprise, we discovered that my previous accountant had failed to file tax returns during my early years living in New York and working as a freelancer. From 2003 to 2005, my income was low, and I had fallen into the habit of not filing my taxes. Looking back, it was a form of denial. I often felt like an imposter, as if my life in New York had not yet fully become real.

When I started my business in 2012, I knew it was important to get everything handled properly. I brought the issue to that accountant and was told that the paperwork had been taken care of. I trusted him. In reality, it had not been resolved, and he had misled me. The earlier returns were never filed, and the IRS eventually filed substitute returns on my behalf based on incomplete information.

My accountant advised me to simply pay the $30,000 bill. In the past, I probably would have accepted that advice without question. I had a long-standing pattern of deferring to perceived authority.

But something in me had changed. I said, "What if we take another approach? I have all the receipts and records from those years. The bill is based on incomplete returns. What if we file the correct ones?"

She warned me that doing so could trigger an audit.

I asked, "What happens in the worst-case scenario?"

"You would still owe the same amount," she replied.

"Then we have nothing to lose," I said. "Let's file the real returns."

That moment marked a shift. For the first time, I fully stepped into my role as the president of my company and advocated for my business.

When the corrected filings were completed, the result was dramatically different. Instead of owing $30,000, I owed $1,000, which I paid immediately.

The experience changed how I understood manifestation. Expansion wasn't about wishing problems away. It required stepping into greater responsibility and leadership. In this case, the next step in my growth wasn't a glamorous breakthrough. It was organizing my finances, addressing unresolved issues, and strengthening my relationship with my accountant.

This became a powerful example of what I call an alchemy item: a challenge that arises during the manifestation process and asks us to become the version of ourselves capable of receiving what we say we want. The transformation wasn't simply about resolving a tax bill. It changed how I viewed the structures supporting my business and my role within them.

From that point forward, I began encouraging the people I work with to adopt an entrepreneurial mindset: to view every experience as information that can help us grow. Instead of asking, "Why is this happening?" I encourage people to ask different questions: *How can I relate to this with curiosity and optimism? How might this be part of everything working out? How can I show up here as the person I am becoming?*

During this time, I codified these techniques and taught others about alchemy items. I introduced a meditation practice that integrated visualization and embodiment to strengthen intention and focus. Research shows that vividly imagining an experience activates many of the same neural systems involved in attention and perception.[3] Visualization can therefore strengthen focus and working memory—the ability to hold and manipulate information in real time—which supports decision-making and problem-solving.[4] When practiced intentionally, imagery can also influence emotional patterns and adaptive coping, helping us respond more skillfully to challenges.[5,6]

Alongside this work, I deepened my understanding of how unwinding is supported through daily reflection. As a mindfulness practice, reflection helps reveal patterns by tracking daily successes and setbacks, allowing insights to be integrated more consciously. Research on mindfulness shows that cultivating present-moment awareness strengthens the ability to observe thoughts, emotions, and behaviors without immediately reacting to them, improving self-regulation and psychological integration.[7,8]

These practices gradually shaped a more integrated approach to business coaching. Instead of asking only how to grow a business, I explored what kind of life, career, or business structure allowed me to function at my best. I realized that when I operate in alignment with my own capacity and well-being, my business thrives as well. This insight reframed my work and deepened my understanding of the BizAttune process.

As my practice developed, I continued to notice how intuition unfolded through real-life experience. Sometimes an idea would arise intuitively, and I would hesitate to trust it

---

3. Pearson, J., Naselaris, T., Holmes, E. A., & Kosslyn, S. M. (2015). Mental imagery: Functional mechanisms and clinical applications. *Trends in Cognitive Sciences, 19*(10), 590–602.https://doi.org/10.1016/j.tics.2015.08.003

4. Keogh, R., & Pearson, J. (2018). The blind mind: No sensory visual imagery in aphantasia. *Cortex, 105*, 53–60. https://doi.org/10.1016/j.cortex.2017.10.012 . Pearson et al., "Mental Imagery,"

5. Holmes, E. A., & Mathews, A. (2010). Mental imagery in emotion and emotional disorders. *Clinical Psychology Review, 30*(3), 349–362. https://doi.org/10.1016/j.cpr.2010.01.001 .

6. Blackwell, S. E., Holmes, E. A., & colleagues. (2015). Mental imagery in emotion and emotional disorders: From cognitive neuroscience to clinical practice. *Nature Reviews Neuroscience, 16*(1), 1–14.

7. Brown, K. W., & Ryan, R. M. (2003). The benefits of being present: Mindfulness and its role in psychological well-being. *Journal of Personality and Social Psychology, 84*(4), 822–848.https://doi.org/10.1037/0022-3514.84.4.822 .

8. Keng, S. L., Smoski, M. J., & Robins, C. J. (2011). Effects of mindfulness on psychological health: A review of empirical studies. *Clinical Psychology Review, 31*(6), 1041–1056. https://doi.org/10.1016/j.cpr.2011.04.006

immediately. Over time, however, people, teachers, and experiences repeatedly appeared that mirrored what I had already been sensing internally.

This became especially clear when I taught the BodyAttune Radiant Human meditation—my heart-based meditation practice—in 2009 alongside the Business Alchemy meditations. Early on, I questioned whether what I was teaching was truly valid. Then I met Juan Li, a Tibetan Buddhist monk visiting New York. After spending a weekend learning from him, I realized he was teaching principles that had already been emerging intuitively in my own work. His training with Tibetan lamas in Nepal echoed ideas I had been discovering on my own. That confirmation strengthened my trust in my inner authority and deepened my commitment to daily practice as both discipline and devotion.

Over time, I saw that what had often felt like self-doubt actually had structure. I was watching what I call "psychic inversion" unwind in real time. For years, my intuition had functioned primarily as a survival mechanism, scanning outward to read environments and anticipate threats to create safety. The subconscious moved toward others rather than inward toward discernment, and clarity often blurred with projection.

The shift did not come from pushing harder. It emerged through structured practice. Working through thirty-, ninety-, and one-hundred-day cycles, I intentionally repatterned my nervous system by reinforcing grounding, clarifying intention, and addressing subconscious conditioning. Gradually, the pattern of using intuition to predict and protect softened, allowing intuition to return to its original orientation as an internal guidance system.

Self-doubt still surfaced occasionally, but it no longer dominated. The co-creative nature of the work produced tangible reassurance. Each aligned outcome strengthened my trust in the process, and encounters with teachers whose language mirrored my own experiences affirmed that my intuition was valid and safe to follow.

Daily practice proved essential during this unwinding phase. As deeper layers surfaced, moments of chaos often accompanied clarity. Returning to intention each day provided stability while those layers reorganized. I celebrated breakthroughs of all kinds—pleasant or uncomfortable—recognizing that awareness itself signaled integration.

Even practical challenges, such as the unexpected tax bill, became part of this recalibration. Gratitude gradually replaced resistance. I partnered with the BizAttune process rather than fighting it and began redefining success. Sacrifice and self-denial were not prerequisites for impact. Nourishment, profitability, and contribution could coexist. To build a conscious business that truly served others, I first had to allow myself to be sustained by it.

Are You Manifesting Correctly?

In Taoism, it is said that where the mind goes is how the energy flows. When the mind aligns with the intention of the absolute, one becomes full of vitality and capable of working with the forces of nature. This is when manifestation becomes alchemy: the practice of applying minimum effort for maximum reward. Being with things as they are and working with what is, rather than what you wish it to be, is considered the highest form of manifestation in Taoist alchemical practice.[9]

In positive psychology, manifestation is often described as the ability to attract success through positive self-talk, visualization, and symbolic action. By thinking positive thoughts, feeling positive emotions, and aligning personal energy with that of the universe, one is said to manifest one's dreams. This differs from many simplified and formulaic "law of attraction" approaches that reduce manifestation to positive thinking alone. I find that people most often become stuck when they overemphasize thinking and neglect feeling or constructive action.

Thought suppression, including forced positive thinking, is associated with increased intrusive thoughts.[10] Overemphasizing positivity can also lead to avoidance patterns that interfere with emotional processing and authentic decision-making. Psychological

9. Kohn, L. (2009). *Daoist meditation and longevity techniques*. Three Pines Press.

10. Wegner, D. M. (1994). Ironic processes of mental control. *Psychological Review, 101*(1), 34–52.

models such as Acceptance and Commitment Therapy describe how attempts to suppress internal experiences often increase distress rather than reduce it.[11]

Being positive expresses itself through constructive action, which reduces rumination and stress reactivity while fostering grounded progress. Constructive action may involve facing avoided feelings, making choices aligned with personal values, placing attention on what is working while practicing gratitude, or engaging in acts of kindness and service. These actions support manifestation not by forcing specific outcomes but by cultivating the internal feeling state aligned with intention—shifting from external fixation to embodied resonance. Research in positive psychology suggests that positive emotions broaden cognitive flexibility and support adaptive coping and resilience.[12]

Curiosity and mindfulness transform manifestation into integration. Each step becomes a movement toward wholeness, where previously unconscious patterns become visible and available for change.[13]

Intention organizes energy. In yogic traditions, this is reflected in the practice of *sankalpa*, an intention planted in the unconscious that aligns conscious desire with deeper spiritual essence.[14] In Tantric understanding, manifestation becomes the attunement of personal will with a broader intelligence guiding experience.[15]

This process is associated with the HRIT chakra, sometimes described as the heart within the heart.

---

11. Hayes, S. C., Strosahl, K., & Wilson, K. (2012). *Acceptance and commitment therapy: The process and practice of mindful change* (2nd ed.). Guilford Press.

12. Fredrickson, B. L. (2001). The role of positive emotions in positive psychology. *American Psychologist, 56*(3), 218–226.

13. Brown, K. W., & Ryan, R. M. (2003). The benefits of being present: Mindfulness and its role in psychological well-being. *Journal of Personality and Social Psychology, 84*(4), 822–848. https://doi.org/10.1037/0022-3514.84.4.822

14. Saraswati, S. S. (2002). *Yoga nidra*. Bihar School of Yoga.

15. Feuerstein, G. (1998). *The yoga tradition*. Hohm Press.

When the HRIT opens, receptivity emerges, and alignment replaces control. The HRIT teaches that leadership is not about micromanaging outcomes but about presence, timing, and trust.

Many high achievers operate primarily from willpower—pushing, striving, and forcing results. While this approach can produce short-term gains, it can also fragment intuitive clarity and exhaust the body. The HRIT offers another orientation. When longing aligns with a larger intelligence of life, the question shifts from "How can I make this happen?" to "What wants to emerge through me?"

Although the HRIT chakra is not a physiological structure, its traditional descriptions can be interpreted alongside modern research on interoception, homeostasis, and heart–brain communication. Some scholars suggest that traditional subtle-body systems function as early phenomenological maps of central nervous system processes involved in interoception, emotional regulation, and meditative awareness.[16]

Contemplative traditions have long described inner awareness practices as ways of perceiving subtle internal signals that guide emotional balance, attention, and decision-making. Modern neuroscience increasingly studies these processes under the concept of "interoception," the brain's perception of internal bodily signals such as heartbeat, breathing, and visceral states, which play an important role in emotion, cognition, and decision-making.[17]

Signals from the body—including cardiovascular signals—are transmitted through neural pathways to the brain and contribute to emotional processing, perception, and behavior.[18] Research on the somatic marker hypothesis suggests that bodily signals help guide intuitive decision-making by providing rapid affective feedback that influences

16. Loizzo, J. J. (2016). The subtle body: An interoceptive map of central nervous system function and meditative mind–brain–body integration. *Annals of the New York Academy of Sciences, 1373*(1), 78–95.

17. Craig, A. D. (2009). How do you feel—now? The anterior insula and human awareness. *Nature Reviews Neuroscience, 10*(1), 59–70.

18. Critchley, H. D., & Garfinkel, S. N. (2017). Interoception and emotion. *Current Opinion in Psychology, 17*, 7–14.

cognitive evaluation before conscious reasoning occurs.[19] Contemporary theories of emotion similarly emphasize the role of interoception in shaping perception, cognition, and the construction of emotional experience.[20]

The vagus nerve, a central component of the autonomic nervous system, carries signals between internal organs and the brain and plays a key role in regulating emotional states and physiological balance.[21] These regulatory processes contribute to the body's capacity to maintain homeostasis and respond adaptively to changing internal and external conditions.

In this context, the HRIT may be understood symbolically as representing the meeting place of physiological regulation, emotional resonance, and intuitive awareness. Rather than literalizing the chakra as an anatomical structure can be viewed as a phenomenological map describing experiences of coordinated heart–brain regulation and embodied awareness.

When autonomic balance and interoceptive awareness improve, individuals often report greater access to intuitive insight and clearer perception of internal signals.[22]

In leadership and decision-making contexts, this heightened sensitivity to internal signals can lead to more accurate pattern recognition, allowing intuitive insight to emerge before conscious reasoning fully articulates the underlying information.

From this space, peak performance becomes grounded in presence rather than pressure. Clarity and creativity flow from alignment. Decisions arise from resonance rather than urgency. Performance becomes sustainable through physiological, emotional, and cognitive coherence.

---

19. Bechara, A., & Damasio, A. (2005). The somatic marker hypothesis: A neural theory of economic decision. *Games and Economic Behavior, 52*(2), 336–372. Damasio, A. (1994). Descartes' error: Emotion, reason, and the human brain. Putnam.

20. Barrett, L. F. (2017). *How emotions are made: The secret life of the brain*. Houghton Mifflin Harcourt.

21. Porges, S. W. (2011). *The polyvagal theory*. Norton.

22. Critchley, H. D., & Garfinkel, S. N. (2017). Interoception and emotion. *Current Opinion in Psychology, 17*, 7–14. https://doi.org/10.1016/j.copsyc.2017.04.020.

To lead from this place is to recognize that we are not isolated creators of change but collaborators within a larger rhythm shaping the unfolding process.

From a psychoneuroimmunology perspective, psychological, neurological, and immune systems function as an interconnected network. Research shows that thoughts, emotions, and stress responses influence hormonal activity, immune function, and overall health.[23,24,25]

Seen through this lens, the chakra system can be understood not as literal anatomy but as a symbolic framework describing patterns of interaction between psychological experience, physiological regulation, and energetic perception. Contemporary reviews of chakra research similarly suggest that chakra models may function as conceptual maps linking subjective experience, physiological processes, and mind–body regulation.[26] When imbalance arises in one domain—emotional, psychological, or physiological—changes often appear in the others as well. When balance returns, coherence ripples outward across the system.

---

23. Ader, R., Felten, D., & Cohen, N. (2001). *Psychoneuroimmunology (*3rd ed.). Academic Press.Houghton Mifflin Harcourt.

24. Barrett, L. F. (2017). *How emotions are made: The secret life of the brain.* Houghton Mifflin Harcourt.

25. McEwen, B. S. (2007). Physiology and neurobiology of stress and adaptation. *Physiological Reviews, 87*(3), 873–904.

26. Moga, M. M. (2022). Is there scientific evidence for chakras? *Cureus, 14*(4), e23895.

Chapter Seven

The Business Alchemy Vortex

By 2017, I faced yet another crossroads. The wonderful space I had been subletting was closing because the building was being sold and demolished. What looked like a practical decision about where to work would eventually prove to be a turning point, a period when the deeper structure of my business methodology revealed itself. I had to make a decision: should I let go of a physical space altogether and work virtually, or should I look for another location?

I ultimately relocated to Union Square, although I wasn't entirely confident in my choice. It felt like a series of synchronous events unfolded when a colleague suggested I check out her building and provided me with the manager's contact information.

I called the manager, and we arranged a time for me to visit the space. However, when I showed up, he didn't remember our appointment, which gave me a sinking feeling that this was going to be a disaster. But then he surprised me by saying, "Why don't we just go look at the space anyway?"

I was astonished. I had expected to discuss the possibility of joining the building, but instead, I found myself actually touring an available office space. When I stepped inside, I was taken aback by how beautiful it was. The office was the perfect size, with large windows overlooking Union Square, providing ample natural light. It was also set back from the park, making it a quiet and serene environment. It felt like the ideal sanctuary.

Before I could fully process my thoughts, I blurted out, “I love this; I’ll take it!” Later, I learned that the current tenants were ending their lease and that I had just happened to visit at the right time. In fact, the manager had already told someone else they could have the space, but he preferred me instead. It all felt destined because everything unfolded so quickly. Nearly a month passed without any updates from the manager. Just when I decided to move forward without a physical office, I checked my email and found a message from him. He confirmed that the space was still available and asked if I wanted it. I immediately accepted the offer.

For the first time, I was looking at my own space—a full-time office all to myself—and I felt I could really expand. I became a little overzealous. Respected colleagues and fellow practitioners started coming to me saying, "I want to work for you. I want to be here." This excitement led me to bring on three practitioners I respected, who used my office on the days I wasn’t working. Everything happened so quickly, and I hadn’t planned for any of it. I had decided to slow down, yet here I was working day and night to market and promote my new team while trying to fill my own schedule—all to fulfill this dream of having my own office space. I was overwhelmed.

Around the same time I expanded into the new office, I reinjured my knee—an old vulnerability I thought I had already strengthened—after playing tennis a little too zealously on a first date with Alex, the man who would one day become my husband. I heard the familiar pop, that unmistakable signal that something had gone wrong. My orthopedic surgeon examined it and told me with certainty that my ACL had ruptured and would need to be replaced.

When I went for the MRI, I joked that with all the magnetism in that machine, maybe I’d tap into the quantum field and repair the ligament myself. I even told Alex, half-serious, half-playing with the idea of spontaneous healing, that the doctor was going to come into the follow-up appointment and announce, “Good news, it’s healed!”

To everyone’s surprise—including my own—that is exactly what he said. Somehow, my ACL was fully intact. I still needed surgery for a meniscus tear and some scar tissue, but the structural stability of the knee was solid. That moment felt like a quiet affirmation of everything I was learning about belief, energy, intention, and the body’s capacity to reorganize itself.

I committed to physical therapy with the same slow-and-steady devotion I was trying to cultivate in my business. I didn't rush the process, and I didn't treat surgery as something to "get through" so I could return to productivity. I treated it as an initiation into a different relationship with my body. Not only did I heal from surgery—I actually strengthened my knee beyond where it had been before the injury. Today, it's the most stable and resilient it has ever been. That healing became a living metaphor for the deeper lesson I was still resisting: slow is sustainable, and sustainable is powerful.

Not long after, my business reflected the same lesson about pacing that my body had just taught me.

The support staff member who was helping me with marketing, a wonderful woman who had done so much for my business, called to say, "This is too hard; I can't do this anymore. I have to let it go." That was a clear signal for me: I had expanded too much, too quickly.

Around the same time, Alex and I took a red-eye to Las Vegas to visit his family. Upon arriving in Vegas, I noticed my body was swollen. I assumed it was the elevation and the overnight flight. However, the swelling persisted throughout our five-day trip and continued when I returned home. I was having trouble sleeping, and my body was still swollen as I struggled to adjust back to my routine.

Despite this, I kept pushing myself hard with marketing and my business launch. Deep down, I couldn't ignore the feeling that something was wrong. Concerned, I scheduled an appointment with a doctor, and during the consultation, my vitals revealed that my kidney function was alarmingly low. My eGFR (which measures how well your kidneys filter blood) was 62 out of 100 percent function—very close to levels associated with stage 2 chronic kidney disease. This revelation was alarming, especially since kidney disease ran in my family.

Slowing down felt like I was letting everyone else down and confirming once again that things just don't work out for me. I believed that if I pulled back, everything I had built would collapse.

I faced another difficult reality: I needed to pull back and focus on my health. My body was sending the same signal it had before: I was pushing again when I needed to slow down. I had to listen.

Around this same period, another set of events forced me to confront my relationship with fear and intuition. I experienced two robberies within the span of a month that unexpectedly deepened my understanding of the difference between fear and intuition.

The first occurred while I was meditating in my office. In the middle of the meditation, I sensed that something was off, but dismissed it as nothing. When I returned home later that evening, the police were outside my building. Our apartment had been broken into, and valuables had been taken, including jewelry and a family heirloom ring my grandmother had given me that once belonged to my late aunt. It turned out our building was part of a larger pattern of break-ins in the neighborhood.

A few weeks later, a second incident unfolded. I was getting ready for a date when I felt a strong inner signal telling me not to go. I convinced myself it was simply fear around a new relationship and decided to override it. Before the date, I planned to attend an outdoor qigong class my teacher hosted in Greenwich Village. Everyone placed their bags on a nearby park bench while we practiced. That made me uneasy, but I pushed the feeling aside.

Within minutes, someone shouted, "He's got your purse!" I looked up and saw a man running away with it. I chased him through the park and down into the subway, nearly catching him as the train doors closed.

Both experiences forced me to examine the tension between intuition and what is often dismissed as fear. In the second instance, my intuition had clearly signaled something, and I ignored it. The question that stayed with me afterward was not whether fear was wrong, but how to distinguish fear from intuition. The answer was not to become less cautious but to become more discerning.

When I reported the theft at the police station, I discovered a room full of people who had experienced similar crimes in the area. The events were not personal. What they revealed instead was the importance of strengthening boundaries—practically, emotionally, and energetically.

At the time, I could not have known whether the signal I felt was intuition offering a warning or simply fear. Through those experiences, however, I came to recognize the difference and what each felt like in my body. They required me to sharpen my discernment, strengthen my boundaries, and learn to trust those signals so that, moving forward, I could respond to them without needing to experience the lesson firsthand.

The timing was striking. Looking back, these events were not isolated incidents but part of the same period of recalibration. My body, my business, and my intuition were all demanding the same thing: a different relationship with pace, safety, and trust.

Both robberies occurred during a period when my business was expanding financially. In a strange way, the events required me to fortify my sense of security before there was even more at stake.

I made the tough calls to the new team members I had hoped to bring on board, informing them that I had to pause the expansion and concentrate on my well-being.

It was during a subsequent energy healing session that I made a shocking connection: the emotion of fear seemed to be directly affecting my kidney function. At first, I assumed these signals were simply a response to the recent stress of being robbed twice. But as the sessions unfolded, I understood that my health issues were rooted in older, deeper wounds. Two significant childhood experiences resurfaced with unexpected intensity: witnessing violence in my neighborhood and a hospital stay, all before the age of three. These memories emerged as tangible, present somatic imprints that were still influencing my physical well-being.

Additionally, within a day of any energy healing session, my gut issues would become much worse. One experience stands out in particular. I had a healing session the day before going on a cruise, then spent two days curled up in my cabin, unable to move, despite having visited the infirmary to rule out appendicitis. My body was writhing in agony, and the dreams were undeniable—I was processing early childhood experiences that had felt trapped my whole life, dislodging from deep in my organs. It was an undeniable connection that created profound shifts in my awareness, validating the deep impact of those early experiences.

That was the moment I knew this wasn't random.

I started researching whether there was a link between chronic kidney disease and gut inflammation. I found a study linking a backup of proteins from the gut to kidney damage.[1] After struggling with long-term digestive issues, I shifted my attention toward healing my gut.

Research on Adverse Childhood Experiences (ACEs) helps explain how chronic stress in childhood is associated with long-term chronic health conditions, including inflammation-related disease. In the landmark ACE Study led by Dr. Vincent Felitti and the CDC, researchers found that chronic stress in childhood creates lasting physiological patterns in the nervous system. Even when early stressors are normalized or forgotten, the body remembers. Elevated ACE scores are associated with a sensitized stress response and heightened inflammation—patterns that can contribute to chronic illness later in life.[2]

I felt like I was onto something, so I began a dual journey of emotional and physical healing. I embraced a mix of meditation, exercise, dietary changes, and traditional therapy, a blend that combined the best of holistic and evidence-based practices.

Understanding this connection helped me release the shame around my reactions and recognize them as adaptive survival patterns rather than personal shortcomings. This scientific lens allowed me to see my patterns not as failures, but as intelligent responses to inherited stress—patterns that could be unwound once brought into conscious awareness.

I pulled back and rested more than I ever had before. Even during the two years when I really downsized, I was resting significantly more and focusing intensely on my health. I made it a priority to go to the gym every day and ensure I was eating the right foods to support my kidney health.

Within a year of embracing holistic healing methods, I witnessed tangible improvements. My kidney function test results dramatically improved, soaring from a concerning 62 to a robust 88 percent of full function for someone my age.

---

1. *Surprising Link Found between Kidney Disease and Gut Inflammation*. (2019, July 10) Columbia Irving Medical Center. https://www.cuimc.columbia.edu/news/surprising-link-found-between-kidney-disease-and-gut-inflammation.

2. Felitti, V. J., Anda, R. F., Nordenberg, D., Williamson, D. F., Spitz, A. M., Edwards, V., Koss, M. P., & Marks, J. S. (1998). Relationship of childhood abuse and household dysfunction to many of the leading causes of death in adults: The Adverse Childhood Experiences (ACE) Study. *American Journal of Preventive Medicine, 14*(4), 245–258. https://doi.org/10.1016/S0749-3797(98)00017-8

What I learned was that the more I rested, the more successful my business became. Without making any extra effort, things just seemed to fall into place. The better I felt, the better my business performed.

Rest was not slowing my business down. It was reorganizing how it worked.

My business vortex process was teaching me that pushing harder was holding me back and that my health and well-being were an integral part of creating the impactful business I envisioned. This was exactly what I had been teaching everyone else in my coaching programs, and I was living it and experiencing it firsthand, which felt incredibly validating. I was beginning to trust the BizAttune process on an even deeper level than I had before.

This experience was yet another indicator of the incredible power of this work to support success in ways one might not typically imagine. I had always envisioned my business as a space where I could grow as a teacher, author, and healer, integrating the various studies I had pursued over the years, including Taoist meditation, yoga, tantric philosophy, and energy healing. I wanted to blend these practices through my business coaching process to help others create a life they don't need to heal from. I saw that working through me. It was a powerful recognition.

It was working, sometimes even in spite of my efforts. I often felt as though I was swimming upstream against everything I was teaching and practicing. Yet, this journey was compelling me to make the necessary changes, almost magnetically pulling me in.

During this transformative period, I decided to take a step towards fulfilling my dream of integration by returning to deep yoga study and practice. I spent a month in Costa Rica three years earlier, and I was feeling ready for the next level of study. I invested in an advanced yoga teacher training program with ISHTA Yoga. I studied at their studio when I first moved to New York. With all the chaos of 9/11 that year, I set my yoga studies aside and never returned to them, but I had always dreamed of studying more deeply with ISHTA.

Now, I felt it was the right time to pursue this goal. I was particularly interested in learning more about the energetics of manifestation, as the teachings at ISHTA are profound in this area. Alan Finger, founder of ISHTA and Tantric Master, played a major role in popularizing yoga in the West. He is the son of Yogi Raj (yoga master). As part of our training, we engaged in an intense period of self-study called "svadhyaya." I chose to study my business alchemy process. I was able to contextualize this process through the lens of tantric philosophy, which allowed me to gain a deeper understanding.

It was amazing to realize that the wisdom flowing through me was connected to this ancient knowledge while also being applicable to contemporary life in New York City in 2019. During my svadhyaya, I meditated on my business and asked it to provide me with a daily intention to focus on. It was as if my business was saying, *"Hey, I can help you even more than you believe. I'll guide you on what to focus on each day."*

I committed to a 100-day practice of meditating on my business every morning, receiving an intention, and observing what unfolded as I held that focus. During this period, my business underwent an incredible transformation, and so did I. I understood the BizAttune process on a deeper level and started integrating those insights into my programs. I also worked with manifestation masters in their mentorship to explore the energetics of this process through the lens of ancient tantric philosophy. It was a truly remarkable time.

Then, in March 2020, COVID hit. I was six months into that year's immersion program with a core group of business alchemy practitioners. I taught them how to receive a daily intention from their business. The insights and awareness they gained were instrumental in navigating the uncertainties of that time, allowing them to make significant leaps in their careers and businesses using these tools. It was an incredible opportunity to foster resilience amid uncertainty.

That's when I started to suggest to my clients that maybe their business is their coach. Just like an Olympic athlete, whose peak performance is unlocked in different ways depending on their unique constitution, talents, and goals, your business knows your best self. It provides experiences and information to guide you toward becoming that version of yourself. My clients and I began working with this concept in remarkable ways.

This period was transformative, and people started asking me to train them. They wanted to be certified in this process, not only to apply it to their own businesses but also to coach others using it. I included this in my intentions, asking myself, *Is this aligned for me? Is this really the next stage of my journey?*

This time was a period of continuation for me. I started with energy work and practices like Pilates, embracing an eclectic approach as a kind of "people whisperer." Gradually, I moved into business coaching, focusing on the energetics of business. Over time, this evolved into my main focus: business coaching centered on business intuition development and the energetics of business. It became clear that this was my path.

I managed my business in this way while also working with others who wished to approach their businesses similarly. This was a time of awakening to business energetics, recognizing that a business itself could act as a coach, guiding me through challenges and experiences. I began to understand that a business functions as a separate energy system, alleviating stress I had been holding within my body. By working separately from my personal stress, I enhanced my intuition, accessed flow states, and remained productive, even through rest. This occurred through energetic coherence and entrainment, allowing my body to return to an optimal state of homeostasis.

I redefined success on a personal level in a world that typically equates success with constant hustle. The more I paid attention to how my body and business responded to rest and pressure, the clearer the underlying pattern became. For me, the more I rested, the better I felt, enabling me to achieve outcomes from a more positive and energized state. Hustle had its place, but "busy-ness" as a badge of honor and a culture of constant striving benefited no one.

My business held this frequency, manifesting outcomes that helped me become the best version of myself. This positive relationship with transformational stress encouraged curiosity and optimism, fostering an entrepreneurial mindset. It was not merely about imagining and creating; the BizAttune process allowed me to embody an authentic entrepreneurial spirit that was uniquely mine.

During this period, I practiced techniques called mirroring and projection. In this context, mirroring meant noticing how external situations reflected internal patterns, while projection required me to examine what I might be attributing to others that actually belonged to me. Instead of pushing outward and grappling with obstacles as problems to control, fix, or solve, I turned inward and focused on how each challenge registered in my body. Working from that internal awareness allowed the stress I had been carrying to release.

This process emphasized sensing, feeling, and embodiment, principles I had first explored during my days in dance therapy. Now it felt like an evolution of that work, applied in partnership with my business so I could show up more present and fully embodied. From that place, my unique gifts flourished, creating space for deeper and more meaningful connection with others.

Through deep study, daily business meditation, and tantric self-inquiry, I learned that my business was its own energetic system with its own intelligence, capable of guiding me, coaching me, and activating my peak performance in ways force never could. This period refined my methodology and marked the true beginning of business energetics as my professional path.

Why a Vortex?

A vortex is a spiraling field of energy that reorganizes how information moves through the mind–body system. It is not symbolic. It is functional. In subtle-energy anatomy, chakras operate in a similar way. They function as vortices that receive, filter, and distribute signals across the nervous, endocrine, and immune networks. From a psychoneuroimmunology perspective, these centers behave like information hubs that regulate perception, stress responses, and overall physiological balance.

When you introduce vortex meditation, you are introducing a coherent spiral field into the biofield—the measurable energetic environment that surrounds and interpenetrates the body.[3,4] As your sphere of awareness expands, perception is no longer confined to surface-level thought. Meditation research shows that sustained attentional training

3. Rubik, B. (2002). The biofield hypothesis: Its biophysical basis and role in medicine. *Journal of Alternative and Complementary Medicine, 8*(6), 703–717. https://doi.org/10.1089/10755530260511711 .

4. Jain, S., Hammerschlag, R., Mills, P., Cohen, L., Krieger, R., Vieten, C., & Lutgendorf, S. (2015). Clinical studies of biofield therapies: Summary, methodological challenges, and recommendations. *Global Advances in Health and Medicine, 4*(Suppl), 58–66. https://doi.org/10.7453/gahmj.2015.118.

increases interoceptive sensitivity and alters perceptual filtering processes in the brain.[5,6] further suggests that traditional subtle body models can be understood as interoceptive maps of central nervous system function, linking embodied awareness with attentional regulation and integration.[7]

The system becomes more sensitive to subtle sensations in the body and to energetic information extending into the surrounding environment. What was previously filtered out as background noise begins to register as meaningful data. Contemporary models of perception and predictive processing indicate that as attentional precision increases, previously suppressed signals can become available to conscious awareness.[8,9] You are not imagining more. You are perceiving more.

That expanded sensitivity supports more accurate sensing, better emotional regulation, and improved intuitive clarity.

Research on focused attention meditation helps explain why. When attention is anchored, neural circuits associated with sustained attention strengthen, while activity linked to distraction and emotional reactivity decreases.[10] Over time, this stabilization

---

5. Farb, N. A. S., Segal, Z. V., & Anderson, A. K. (2013). Mindfulness meditation training alters cortical representations of interoceptive attention. *Social Cognitive and Affective Neuroscience, 8*(1), 15–26. https://doi.org/10.1093/scan/nss066 .

6. Tang, Y.-Y., Hölzel, B. K., & Posner, M. I. (2015). The neuroscience of mindfulness meditation. *Nature Reviews Neuroscience, 16*(4), 213–225. https://doi.org/10.1038/nrn3916.

7. Loizzo, J. J. (2016). The subtle body: an interoceptive map of central nervous system function and meditative mind–brain–body integration. *Annals of the New York Academy of Sciences, 1373*(1), 78–95. https://doi.org/10.1111/nyas.13065

8. Clark, A. (2013). Whatever next? Predictive brains, situated agents, and the future of cognitive science. *Behavioral and Brain Sciences, 36*(3), 181–204. https://doi.org/10.1017/S0140525X12000477 .

9. Seth, A. K. (2013). Interoceptive inference, emotion, and the embodied self. *Trends in Cognitive Sciences, 17*(11), 565–573. https://doi.org/10.1016/j.tics.2013.09.007

10. Brefczynski-Lewis, J. A., Lutz, A., Schaefer, H. S., Levinson, D. B., & Davidson, R. J. (2007). Neural correlates of attentional expertise in long-term meditation practitioners. *Proceedings of the National Academy of Sciences, 104*(27), 11483–11488. https://doi.org/10.1073/pnas.0606552104 .

reduces attentional lapses and increases sensitivity to incoming information, enabling more precise detection and response rather than reflexive, conditioned reactions.[11]

The vortex operates in a similar way, with the added effect of organizing coherence across the entire perceptual field.

How the Vortex Disrupts Old Filters

During practice, the vortex acts as a purposeful disruptor. Its coherent movement helps dissolve outdated neural and perceptual patterns so the system can process information with greater precision.

Recent work suggests that the claustrum dynamically modulates activity in prefrontal and cortical networks, enhancing the flexibility and synchronization of neuronal responses involved in attention and integrative processing and may act as an integrative hub contributing to aspects of conscious awareness.[12, 13]

The claustrum integrates signals from the body and environment into a coherent sense of awareness. In contemplative traditions, this integrative field of internal awareness is sometimes described as the "subtle body." As Loizzo argues, the subtle body can be understood not as a mystical structure but as a functional, interoceptive map of central nervous system activity—a way of organizing how internal bodily signals, emotional states, and self-related processing are experienced and regulated.[14]

---

11. MacLean, K. A., Ferrer, E., Aichele, S. R., Bridwell, D. A., Zanesco, A. P., Jacobs, T. L., King, B. G., Rosenberg, E. L., Sahdra, B. K., Shaver, P. R., Wallace, B. A., Mangun, G. R., & Saron, C. D. (2010). Intensive meditation training improves perceptual discrimination and sustained attention. *Psychological Science, 21*(6), 829–839. https://doi.org/10.1177/0956797610371339

12. Atilgan, H., Town, S. M., Wood, K. C., Jones, G. P., Maddox, R. K., Lee, A. K. C., & Bizley, J. K. (2025).*Modulation of prefrontal and cortical network activity by the claustrum supports flexible attention and integrative processing*. Nature Neuroscience.

13. Liaw, Y. S. (2023). The claustrum and consciousness: An update. Brain Research Bulletin.

14. Loizzo, "The Subtle Body."

Over time, however, this integrative system becomes shaped by old assumptions, survival strategies, and habituated interpretations. The way information is synthesized reflects what the system has learned to expect.

The vortex loosens those ingrained synthesis patterns.

As coherence increases, the system begins to reorganize itself. Neuroplasticity improves, meaning that the brain's capacity to form new neural pathways and update old ones strengthens. Communication between body and subtle-body signals and conscious awareness becomes clearer. Intuitive filters refine. Outdated perceptual biases begin to release. The internal maps that once governed interpretation update, making space for new possibilities.

This is not forcing change. It is unburdening what has been shaping perception from beneath awareness.

What the Vortex Activates

As the vortex moves through key energetic regions, it helps awaken and stabilize deeper aspects of the energy architecture that support coherence. When these structures come online, the mind–body network processes information in a more fluid and integrated way.

Flow states become more accessible—creativity and insight increase. Emotional adaptability improves. Physiological regulation stabilizes. A grounded sense of clarity and orientation begins to replace reactivity.

Visualization-based meditation contributes directly to this shift. When you visualize an object, the insula becomes more active. The insula governs interoception, your awareness of subtle body sensations. As insular activation increases, embodied perception deepens, supporting more intuitive and less reactive forms of awareness.[15]

15. Farb, N. A. S., Segal, Z. V., & Anderson, A. K. (2013). Mindfulness meditation training alters cortical representations of interoceptive attention. Social Cognitive and Affective Neuroscience, 8(1), 15–26. https://doi.org/10.1093/scan/nss066 . Seth, "Interoceptive Inference."

Why It Matters

The vortex creates the conditions under which transformation becomes natural, without forcing anything.

As coherence increases within the biofield and communication between subconscious signaling and conscious awareness improves, a more integrated intelligence emerges.[16] Perception becomes less shaped by past conditioning and more aligned with present-moment accuracy.[17] Decision-making becomes less burdened by inherited stress patterns. Emotional regulation stabilizes not through suppression, but through integration.

The vortex becomes a reliable internal stabilizing field. It supports clearer perception, healthier decision-making, and expanded access to insight and possibility without overexertion.

---

16. Rubik, "The Biofield Hypothesis." Jain et al., "Clinical Studies of Biofield Therapies."Loizzo, "The Subtle Body."

17. Clark, "Whatever Next?"

The Science Behind the Effect

Across neuroscience, psychology, and contemplative science, research consistently demonstrates that meditating on a single focus produces measurable changes in attentional control, perceptual processing, interoceptive awareness, and emotional regulation, while also altering how the brain filters and interprets incoming information.[18]

These mechanisms map directly onto what the vortex facilitates: the dissolution of old patterns, increased flow states, and improved communication between conscious and subconscious layers of awareness.[19]

Object-focused meditation reorganizes how the brain filters information.[20] Visualization practices increase interoceptive sensitivity.[21] Together, they support the deeper coherence and clarity the vortex is designed to activate.

18. Brefczynski-Lewis et al., "Neural Correlates of Attentional Expertise."Tang et al., "The Neuroscience of Mindfulness Meditation," Farb et al., "Attending to the Present," Rubik, "The Biofield Hypothesis," Jain et al., "Clinical Studies of Biofield Therapies."

19. Loizzo, "The Subtle Body."

20. Brefczynski-Lewis et al., "Neural Correlates of Attentional Expertise." Clark, "Whatever Next?"

21. Farb et al., "Attending to the Present." Seth, "Interoceptive Inference."

Chapter Eight

Codifying Business Energetics

After years of learning to balance self-care with business growth, I was ready for meaningful expansion—and I wanted to do it the right way. The work I had been developing through years of practice was beginning to take shape as a system, and I knew it was time to give it a structure that could be studied, tested, and taught. In 2020, I wanted to provide an evidence base for the method I'd codified over the years and integrate it into a training program. My goal was to integrate a structure that would genuinely benefit individuals seeking to be trained—not just give them "a piece of paper" and send them on their way. That's why I developed an International Coaching Federation (ICF) certified program. I wanted participants to earn a coaching credential that would be professionally recognized and allow them to connect with a community for ongoing support beyond my guidance alone.

To accomplish this, I explored various graduate programs. I interviewed with several schools, and most admissions teams responded with enthusiasm. My experience in Pilates, dance, yoga, and energy work, coupled with my education in anatomy, kinesiology, and health, made me an attractive candidate. Interviewers warned me that I might find their programs lacking in depth and engagement. They felt I would be a valuable addition to their cohorts, but most master's programs in coaching at the time were geared toward subject areas where I already had significant knowledge. I was looking for something more dynamic.

I briefly attended acupuncture school in 2011 while navigating the end of a six-year relationship. Eager to expand my knowledge and career, I enrolled for a year and enjoyed the experience. However, juggling that intense breakup alongside starting my business proved overwhelming, leading me to take a break from the program. Though I never returned, I always had a fondness for the school and found myself occasionally checking their website.

During one of these visits, I discovered the school had launched a Master of Science in Health and Human Performance degree—an ICF-accredited coaching program. It almost felt too good to be true. Excited, I scheduled an interview with the dean and admissions director. I shared my intention to research and codify my coaching methodology, establish an evidence-based foundation, and use my studies as an opportunity to develop my own coach training program.

The Dean was supportive and encouraging, assuring me that I could tailor all assignments to align with my program development. Inspired and motivated, I decided to enroll, and it turned out to be an amazing journey. I immediately felt at home. I have always longed for a positive, uplifting, and supportive learning environment. This program embodied those core values through its focus on constructive and positive feedback, community, and mutual support.

During my first semester, I faced writing a lot of literature reviews and academic papers. This workload reminded me of my undergraduate days as a research assistant studying visual and auditory perception. All those experiences came rushing back to me as I pulled all-nighters and engaged in endless research. In the first few weeks of grad school, I really stressed myself out. Then I remembered that I had acquired new tools; I was no longer the same student I had been in my early 20s.

During a chaotic period when my logical, left-brain decision-making felt overwhelming, I tapped into my business intuition and allowed my vortex to guide me through feeling and trust. I worked backward from the ideal outcome.

Before writing a paper, I would do an alchemy item meditation and align with the timeline where I had already received an A on the assignment. Then I would broadcast that feeling of success like a lighthouse casting light onto the assignment, attuning it and clearing interference so I could work efficiently, in flow, and in the zone. From that state, I would ask, *What does the perfect paper for this assignment look like? Where can I find the necessary resources?* Then I would outline, edit, and complete the work. Instead of forcing ideas, I remembered how I got there and took those steps.

Working from that state alleviated much of the mental effort. Instead of forcing outcomes, I stayed present, adaptable, and grounded in flow. My work shifted from exhausting all-nighters and producing subpar papers to achieving better grades and higher-quality work. It made achieving my goals more manageable and enjoyable. I applied these strategies in real-life scenarios involving time pressure and performance, making grad school a truly enjoyable experience.

Part of my time in grad school was dedicated to developing my coaching method and obtaining my own coaching certification. To qualify for my exam through the ICF, I needed to log paid coaching hours to meet specific requirements and levels of credentialing. I was unsure how I would accomplish this while being a full-time grad student and running my business.

Throughout this entire process, I was terrified that my business would fail and that I would have to drop out of grad school. I feared not finishing my degree, just as I hadn't completed acupuncture school or other endeavors I had tried over the years. There were courses I took where I didn't graduate, or it took me two years to finally pass the exam and obtain my certification.

During grad school, I was managing eight different programs, including an Introduction and Mastermind group for Business Alchemy, while also working one-on-one with clients. I also began teaching Reiki courses and offering a certification program for my meditation practices. Juggling so many responsibilities felt overwhelming.

My personal life was now fulfilling. My relationship, which had begun in 2017, started to deepen. We talked about marriage, and I felt like my life was improving in every conceivable way. I managed it all by using my vortex.

When my friends would ask, "How are you doing all of that?"

I would respond, "I just use my vortex."

They would roll their eyes, tired of hearing about it, or give me curious looks, wondering what the heck I was talking about.

During this challenging period, I discovered what truly worked for me. The vortex helped ground me and provided the energy to quickly shift from one mindset to another, whether I was in class, working on assignments, or being present with a client or in a group program. It held an outcome that exceeded my imagination, allowing me to let go of my expectations and simply trust the BizAttune process. My vortex was my coach, supporting me to become the version of myself capable of sustaining the outcomes I desired.

Something fundamental had shifted within me. While I received support from various sources during this time, the key element that organized everything for my success was my vortex. My vortex acted as a guide, helping me navigate challenges as they arose. When I made a misstep, it showed me how to reconcile my mistakes and manage my energy throughout the journey. At times, it felt like I was surfing, with my vortex as my surfboard, riding the waves of change.

I experienced daily ups and downs, questioning whether it was truly working or if I was just imagining it. But I could see the proof in the consistent progress I'd made. I've shared many examples from my past, showcasing how hard I pushed, only to find that slowing down was what actually increased my results. What I've realized is that when there's a need to speed up and expand, the BizAttune process supports that, and when it's time to slow down, it provides that support as well. It feels almost magnetic and organic, like a natural rhythm.

During this time, I was also apprenticing with an energy healer, Cyndi Dale, who had given me a reading about my Cherokee lineage. She taught me that my work was to help people understand that accomplishing their goals could be easier than they imagined. I had been studying with her since 2017, continually learning her techniques and understanding her approach to energy and manifestation.

In 2021, she invited me to be a teaching assistant in her year-and-a-half-long energy healing certification program, called the "Four Pathways." Not only was this right in the middle of my graduate program, but I had recently gotten engaged and was planning a wedding. This was a time when the BizAttune process was supporting my active schedule.

The teaching assistant role allowed me to mentor a diverse group of practitioners from around the world, which furthered my commitment to making a global impact. I was also a student in the program. It was an incredible privilege and a profound experience. I managed all of this while going through significant personal and professional expansion, something I never could have planned for or believed I was capable of managing. Throughout this immersion process with Cyndi, we delved deeper into the methods she used, similar to how Juan Li had previously guided me.

Together, we explored some of the psychic inversion patterns that had been emerging in my life, aiming to understand them more profoundly. This understanding would empower me to master my energy and manifest my visions with greater ease. A key focus was on two primary patterns I was encouraged to study. The first was ancestral trauma, which suggested that some of the psychic inversion I experienced could be adaptations inherited from my ancestors. This included coping mechanisms related to stress and safety that are now better understood through epigenetics and environmental sensitivity research, which shows how inherited stress adaptations can contribute to heightened perceptual sensitivity in some individuals.

Additionally, I received guidance through my business alchemy meditation practice to study patterns of narcissism to build my resilience. Understanding these patterns would help me recognize and avoid exploitative people and circumstances that would disrupt my momentum. I had to build this awareness to get where I wanted to be with my career and impact.

This was usually the point where the familiar pattern in my life would take over: just as something was beginning to work, it would fall apart at the last minute. But this time, it didn't fall apart; I developed a clearer understanding of my energetic landscape and began creating a life and structure that supported me through instability as I transitioned into new experiences.

Once in grad school, I focused my research on the neuroscience of change, seeking to validate, from a scientific standpoint, the experiences I had encountered. It's important to note that you don't need to subscribe to tantric or Taoist philosophies to reap their benefits. I aimed to extract wisdom from these ancient practices and translate it into a context that is accessible to everyone. My goal was to adapt these insights into business alchemy, emphasizing the importance of allowing one's intentions, rather than predefined notions of success, to catalyze personal and professional transformation.

This method can accelerate progress in areas where one feels stuck, revealing new possibilities. During this period of mentorship and research in graduate school, I was able to evolve and adapt these concepts for broader use. I learned to trust in the

BizAttune process and let it develop further than I ever anticipated. Additionally, I had the opportunity to create and facilitate a continuing education healing series on trauma and intuition.

This was when I began teaching and educating others about post-traumatic growth, the positive changes that can occur when confronting adversity, while simultaneously pursuing my master's degree and researching the evidence base for the programs I had been offering for years. Recognizing the demand from those who had experienced their benefits firsthand, I formalized these programs more fully.

Yet this was during a time when I didn't believe I had it in me. If someone had told me that I would be doing what I'm doing now, I would have thought they were crazy. I had just gone through a kidney healing experience and other challenging situations, and I believed the BizAttune process was about slowing down. The idea of speeding up seemed like self-sabotage, completely contrary to everything I had learned. Yet, the process seemed to assist me in doing just that, often without my realization until later.

When Guidance Isn't What You Want to Hear

For me, one of those moments came when my inner guidance said that to break through my current struggles and limitations, I needed to understand and explore narcissism. At first, I resisted. I don't believe in rigid labels or diagnoses, and like many, I tend to shy away from subjects that seem to cast judgment or create divisions. The idea of labeling someone a narcissist felt damning, and I wanted to believe in people's capacity for growth and transformation.

At first, it felt unrelated to my work. But as I grew into new levels of visibility and leadership, the guidance became unmistakable. To become the person I was trying to grow into, I needed to understand these relational dynamics more clearly, not to label anyone, but to remain sovereign and grounded in environments where power, projection, and need often intersect.

In business, especially in service-based fields, I encountered patterns I did not yet have language for. They showed up differently from the client dynamics I already understood.

In the professional world, they often appeared as opportunism wrapped in connection. People praised my work lavishly, expressed deep admiration, or framed themselves as aligned collaborators, only to pivot toward soliciting my business, my network, or my revenue. Some said exactly what they thought I needed to hear, positioning themselves as the missing piece to my success. When results did not match their promises, the responsibility quietly shifted back onto me. Others celebrated my wins publicly, liking every post and cheering loudly, while privately angling for what association with me could provide. None of this was malicious. It was simply human behavior amplified by an industry hungry for momentum.

Without understanding the deeper pattern, it was destabilizing. One moment I was idealized. The next, dismissed or blamed. It took time to recognize that what felt personal was often structural, part of a broader cycle where charisma can be mistaken for credibility and connection can be used as currency. My guidance was not warning me about people. It was teaching me how to navigate complexity without losing myself.

The energy-healing world carried its own version of this dynamic. There were hierarchies, spoken and unspoken, where visibility sometimes outweighed integrity. I watched people rise not through mastery, but through competition, performance, and comparison. There was more ego than embodiment, more "spiritual branding" than spiritual practice. It created a strange dissonance. Healing work is meant to dissolve hierarchy, yet the field can easily reproduce the same structures people are trying to leave behind. I often felt out of place because what mattered most to me was not status or recognition, but the quiet, real transformation happening in the room.

What made all of this even more challenging was how deeply the external patterns mirrored my internal ones. I began tapping into the positive shadow of the sovereign as a counterpoint to the martyr, the part of me willing to give endlessly, to hold the weight of others' expectations, to overfunction, and then to be judged for the very overfunctioning that benefitted everyone involved.

I had shaped an identity around being dependable, accommodating, and self-sacrificing, while quietly carrying the cost in my own system. And of course, my clients reflected this back to me. They arrived exhausted, over-responsible, and stretched thin, mirroring the parts of me that were still trying to earn belonging through overgiving.

Moving beyond that pattern required accessing a different part of myself. The version of me capable of holding my energy, practicing radiant leadership, and setting loving boundaries so I could remain sovereign without abandoning myself or the vision I was carrying.

At the same time, I saw many entrepreneurs chasing extrinsic markers not only in their business, from followers, for visibility, and revenue, but also in their inner work. "Opening a chakra," "releasing a block," and "activating abundance codes" became spiritual equivalents of performance metrics. The striving never stopped. It simply shifted realms. But the states they were chasing—clarity, openness, and expansion—are not achievements to be unlocked. They are physiological and energetic conditions that arise naturally when the system is safe, regulated, and given space to rest. I learned through my own body that deep rest and contemplative practice open more inner doors than any technique applied to a stressed system.

My understanding of narcissistic dynamics was not purely intellectual. Years earlier, I had lived through a relationship marked by the very patterns I was now recognizing professionally. At the time, I did not know the language of narcissistic abuse. I only knew that something in me stayed small, compliant, and emotionally overextended. It was not until four years after the relationship ended, long after the external rupture, that I finally understood what I had been navigating. Only then did the healing truly begin.

What surprised me most was how uncomfortable that healing made certain people in my life. My unhealed state had made me accessible, relatable, and useful. My healing disrupted those roles. It revealed how much of my relational life had been built around versions of me that no longer existed.

Understanding these dynamics did not make me cynical. It made me clear. The guidance I received was not about learning to protect myself from others but about learning to stop abandoning myself. It showed me how to remain sovereign and grounded in spaces where projection, urgency, and need can easily blur boundaries and how to stay aligned with my purpose without getting entangled in roles I was never meant to play.

Chapter Nine

Ancestral Patterns and the Unfinished Home

In the alchemical sense, your business forms its own sacred circle with you. It holds a field of coherence that "coaches" you toward the version of yourself capable of fulfilling its potential. Sometimes the lessons it brings forward are not new challenges at all, but unfinished patterns that began long before we were aware of them. My business repeatedly presented circumstances designed to help me grow—not to punish me, but to prepare me. Laura Day—a professional intuitive with whom I studied intuition skills for business directly—calls this the intuitive feedback loop of business psychic work: your business knows when you are aligned, and it knows when you are not.[1]

On a superficial level, this can be seen as "eustress," pushing me out of my comfort zone and helping me align my habits and mindset with the life I aspire to lead.

Initially, I was unaware of these patterns; they had been part of my life for as long as I can remember. As I grew more consciously aware of them, I explored the historical context that shaped these patterns. I uncovered an early childhood experience that became a pivotal imprint on my expectations regarding the process of growth and development.

When I was around six years old, my parents built their dream house. Prior to this, my father held a job that required him to travel frequently, which meant he was often away

1. Day, L. (2009). The Circle: How the Power of a Single Wish Can Change Your Life. Atria Paperback.

from home. Eventually, he expressed a desire to be home more and to spend quality time with us. Rather than renting a home, he wanted to build a home where we could grow up and make lasting memories.

My entire family was involved. My grandfather, who was a carpenter, came to help, and we all worked together. My brother and I dug, explored, and played in the fields and woods around the property while the adults built the house. I would skip Saturday morning cartoons just to be a part of it. The plan was to construct the basement first, move into it, and then build the rest of the house while living in the basement. This was meant to save money and reduce the burden of a mortgage.

I remember the blueprint for our house. "Isn't it going to be beautiful? This is going to be worth it when we're done," we would say. This was part of our motivation as we imagined this amazing A-frame house we were going to build.

We all had that expectation of how incredible it would be once finished. Even at six years old, I understood that it was worth the sacrifice to give up nights and weekends to build our dream home. I helped out on weekends and after school for a year and a half, between the ages of six and eight.

However, around the time we were finishing and putting on the roof, mortgage interest rates skyrocketed. My dad crunched the numbers and decided that if he finished the house at that point, we would be paying for it for the rest of our lives. So, he made the difficult decision not to finish the A-frame house.

As a child, I didn't fully grasp what was happening; I just accepted that we weren't going to proceed. However, over time, this experience left a significant imprint on me: I learned that no matter how hard you work, something unexpected can come along and derail everything.

This early childhood experience shaped my belief that things don’t work out for me. I would see things go well for others, and when they didn’t work out for me, it felt like that was just how life was. It wasn’t until I started working through these feelings that I recognized this pattern.

This was one of the earliest signs of the psychic inversion pattern that shaped how my efforts played out as I worked toward my goals. During that time, I learned to brace for disruption and internalized the belief that everything I worked so hard for could disappear just as it was coming together. Untangling that imprint became essential to breaking the cycle of nearing completion in my own projects, only to watch things collapse.

As an adult, I questioned why my father was so afraid to take out a mortgage. It was such a big deal for him, while many other people took out even high-interest mortgages. My father had a good job and made decent money. Why was this so significant for him?

I find this concept particularly meaningful when I reflect on my family's history. My grandparents came of age during the Great Depression, facing profound scarcity and severe financial difficulties. They gathered herbs to sell and survived periods of time when food was unreliable. Their nervous systems learned vigilance, frugality, and constant alertness—traits necessary for survival in their world.

After the Great Depression, my grandparents developed a profound fear of debt. There's a saying in my family: If you have debt, it's as if you don't own it. When my grandparents first married and bought their house, they went to a furniture store to purchase a bed on credit. After sleeping in it for just one night, they felt uncomfortable, as if they were sleeping in someone else's bed. The next day, they returned to the store and paid off the debt.

This mindset became a defining trait of our family. My father grew up in a household shaped by this fear of debt, and he understood the risks involved. As a result, he adopted the same values and worked to build his house without incurring any debt, paying for everything as he went along with whatever money he had. When it came time for him to take out a mortgage, my father just couldn't bring himself to do it. It was more than just a rational decision; it was the fears of his ancestors coming through him.

The ripple effect of this decision on my life has been enormous. I've spent time unpacking these feelings and learning how to have a healthy relationship with money. I've realized that there is such a thing as good debt. I genuinely believe that I would not have reached this understanding without going through the BizAttune process.

As I delved deeper into these thoughts, I came to understand that when we face adversities that echo the struggles of our ancestors, our emotional responses can feel outsized—almost as if we're reliving something we never personally lived. Emerging research in neuroscience and epigenetics offers insight into why.

Neuroscientist Bianca Jones Marlin describes this inherited sensitivity as "a biological mechanism for survival," noting that the body can carry forward information about danger so that descendants are better prepared. In her now well-known mouse experiments, adult mice were exposed to the smell of almonds paired with a mild foot shock. They learned to fear that scent. What is remarkable is what happened next: "Their offspring, who had never encountered the shock, still displayed an exaggerated fear response to the almond odor." Marlin's team found these descendants were born with more smell receptors for detecting that specific scent, and even the regions of their brain associated with olfaction were structurally altered.

Researchers believe this inherited sensitivity moves through "epigenetic marks"—chemical tags on DNA that adjust how genes are expressed without changing the genetic code itself. As Marlin explains, "Our experiences can write themselves into our biology."[2]

Human research echoes this. Rachel Yehuda, a leading researcher on intergenerational trauma, found that women who were pregnant during the September 11 attacks and developed PTSD showed altered cortisol patterns, the hormone involved in stress regulation. Their infants also showed corresponding differences in cortisol early in life. Yehuda has emphasized that this is not simply psychological transmission but biological—trauma can alter the gestational environment in ways that shape the baby's stress response even before birth.[3]

Her work with families of Holocaust survivors similarly shows that descendants can exhibit altered stress responses, including changes in cortisol regulation, suggesting that the effects of trauma can extend across generations.[4] Her research emphasizes that these inherited patterns are not fixed outcomes, but starting points that can be understood and transformed.

---

2. Marlin, B. J. (2024). Inherited trauma and the biology of stress transmission. STAT News.https://www.statnews.com/2024/04/12/bianca-jones-marlin-columbia-inherited-trauma-stress/

3. Yehuda, R., & Bierer, L. M. (2009). The relevance of epigenetics to PTSD: Implications for the DSM-V. Journal of Traumatic Stress, 22(5), 427–434. https://doi.org/10.1002/jts.20448

4. Yehuda, R., Schmeidler, J., Wainberg, M., Binder-Brynes, K., & Duvdevani, T. (1998). Vulnerability to posttraumatic stress disorder in adult offspring of Holocaust survivors. American Journal of Psychiatry, 155(9), 1163–1171. https://doi.org/10.1176/ajp.155.9.1163

This helped me understand why I reacted not only to my personal history but also to patterns carried through family and cultural inheritance. Jung described how individuals can be especially sensitive to collective material, and I came to see this sensitivity as a kind of receptivity to unresolved patterns held within families and environments. In practical terms, this means we may register emotional imprints transmitted across generations or embedded in the systems we grow up in. If your ancestors experienced collapse, scarcity, or instability, your system may still carry echoes of those experiences as if they were your own. This sensitivity is often heightened among intuitive practitioners, healers, and Highly Sensitive Persons (HSPs).

Understanding epigenetic inheritance helps me recognize how echoes of my ancestors' experiences may live in my own body—why certain financial stressors can feel amplified and why my system sometimes reacts as if collapse is imminent, even when safety is present. It's not about repeating the past, but about understanding how deeply the past can shape the foundation we rise from.What I later learned is that this doesn't only come through inheritance. It's also shaped through how we neurologically learn and relate. Mirror neurons are a network of brain cells that help us understand others by internally simulating their actions and emotions, forming a biological foundation for empathy, learning, and social connection. They prime us to feel and internalize the emotional states of those around us, especially in childhood. Jung spoke of this through the lens of the collective unconscious. Empaths often absorb unresolved collective material as if it were their own. This explained why I felt financial collapse in my body long before it showed up in my bank account.

Over time I found that strengthening my intuition by holding a clear intention acted as a stabilizer for my nervous system. Instead of using intuition to "listen for danger," I began using it to create my reality, re-patterning the stress response from survival into possibility.

In energy medicine traditions, persistent emotional and relational patterns are sometimes described as energetic "cords" linking us to unresolved family dynamics.[5] In many ways, this language parallels what epigenetic research suggests biologically—that the effects of stress and experience can be transmitted across generations, shaping how the body responds to the world. Seen through that lens, I recognized how my own system had

5. Eden, D., & Feinstein, D. (2008). Energy medicine. TarcherPerigee. Dale, C. (2009). The subtle body: An encyclopedia of your energetic anatomy. Sounds True.

inherited what felt like energetic contracts—agreements to carry what others could not metabolize.

This helped explain why I often felt responsible for holding things together or "taking on" the emotional or financial burdens of others, even at my own expense. What we inherit from our lineage is never only the wound. It also includes the wisdom that allowed our ancestors to survive it. Inheritance is not limited to burdens; we also inherit gifts.

As my work deepened and the patterns around scarcity and instability unwound, I noticed something unexpected emerge. Although I had always been drawn to creative expression through writing and dance, the BizAttune process activated another lineage within my family. Several members of my family are business owners and naturally skilled with numbers, economics, and financial planning. As the system shifted toward constructive manifestation, those ancestral strengths surfaced alongside the creative and healing gifts I had already cultivated.

We all experience similar patterns. Each of us carries unique ancestral influences shaped by culture, family upbringing, and life experience, all of which shape how we respond to stress and opportunity. Through the BizAttune process, it becomes possible to unwind inherited stress patterns while reclaiming the talents and capacities that were always part of our lineage. As those patterns reorganize, what once felt like a burden can become a source of stability and support for the work we are here to do.

Now, when I feel resistance or fear, I recognize it as my ancestors speaking through me. They adapted to survive and passed that adaptation down to me. I can consciously recognize and acknowledge that this is an ancestral fear arising, and instead of rejecting it, I can lovingly embrace it and choose a different path.

I never intended to become a business coach focused on business energetics. But my business had its own blueprint for health. Part of that blueprint involved me stepping into the role of a business coach to unpack and heal my relationship with money. I believe my business was there to help me heal these ancestral patterns.

Even if money isn't your primary goal, it always serves as the organizing principle, or consciousness, of your business. For a venture to truly be classified as a business, money must play a central role; otherwise, it is just a hobby.

I've shared numerous stories about how this has manifested in my experiences. As my business creates opportunities for me to grow with sustainable energy of success, it has allowed me to evaluate my relationship with money, my fear of debt, my fear of abundance, and the ways I hold back due to the fear of failure and poor financial management.

This is when the difference between manifestation and alchemy became clear to me. Manifestation describes the outcome; alchemy describes the transformation that makes the outcome possible. The work was not simply about thinking differently—it was about updating the filters through which my nervous system interpreted reality. That's what reprograms the unconscious blueprint and shifts the trajectory of your business.

This unconscious programming has led to experiences that reveal I am skilled at business and capable of helping others move past their blocks to discover new ways of relating to success that they hadn't considered.

With each breakthrough my clients achieve, I shift further into that place of confidence.

This is why I say that successful work is not manifestation in the trendy sense—it's alchemy. It requires transforming the inner structure that creates your reality, not forcing the outcome. When you change the blueprint, the results evolve naturally.

Meditation, energetic alchemy, and the vortex practice reoriented my system from collapse to creation. These tools update the unconscious filters through which reality is interpreted, shifting the body from reacting to the past to generating a new future.

For example, one of my coaching clients came to me expressing her struggles. She said she had worked with many other coaches and energy healers but consistently overspent. She shared that, after investing heavily in her personal development, she often found herself on the brink of bankruptcy, fearing she might lose everything. Despite her fears, she turned to me because she believed I could offer a different path.

I structured our coaching relationship to span a year, sensing that she had complex dynamics that would take time to work through. Her parents had experienced bankruptcies, which created a lack of stability in her upbringing. As an adult, she needed to learn how to establish security for herself, overcoming many of the coping mechanisms she had developed in an unstable environment.

My client expressed that she was tired of supporting other people's success. She was exceptionally skilled in marketing, social media, and online advertising, helping many practitioners build successful six- and seven-figure businesses. However, she was ready to focus on her own success. Having studied energy healing, she felt passionate about it and wanted to transition from being a marketer to becoming a healer in her own business.

I asked her, "What will success look like when you're running your energy healing business full-time and no longer working in marketing for someone else? Why do you want that for yourself?" I encouraged her to explore what was important and valuable to her.

She replied, "I am passionate about this work. I want to help people, but I also see the success I create for others, and I need similar financial returns. I'm a single mother, and I have health issues. It's difficult to give fully to others without neglecting myself on some level. I'm worried about being able to continue working to provide for my daughter. I have a mortgage and debt. I want to pay off my mortgage, eliminate my debt, and gain more freedom to say yes or no to commitments, allowing me to care for myself because I want to be present for my daughter. As I get older and she starts her own family, I want to be there for that. It's incredibly important to me."

I completely understood her priorities. She had a clear vision of where she wanted to be; it was just a matter of closing the gap between her current situation and her goals. We began by assessing her bills and budget, determining how much she needed to earn and what she should be charging.

We crunched the numbers to find out the minimum amount she needed to make to set herself on this path and allow for future growth. We worked through all of this together and meditated on her intended outcome. We visualized her success, envisioning the moment she reached her goals.

I took her through the following exercise: "I want you to allow your body to experience what that feels like. Take a moment to visualize yourself in a place where you've already succeeded. You're healthy. Your bills are paid. You're earning a good income doing something you love. You no longer worry about your health. You feel vibrant and fully capable of supporting your daughter. What does that feel like? What sensations arise in your body?"

What unfolded in our work together was a recognition that her exhaustion, overspending, and fear of collapse were not personal failures—they were her nervous system's way of adapting because it had never been taught how to feel safe. She had spent years trying to outrun the instability of her childhood by doing more, giving more, and demanding more of herself. But no amount of effort could override the underlying overwhelm in her body.

When you begin overworking to compensate for a setback, your system shifts into a chronic "doing mode." At first, it looks like skipping rest here and there. Over time, it becomes the inability to rest at all. Even when you finally give yourself permission to slow down—take a weekend away, clear your calendar, go on vacation—you don't feel restored. Your system doesn't recognize the "off switch" anymore.

That's because once the body gets locked into the stress pathway, it interprets slowing down as a threat.[6] Bandwidth is already maxed out, so shifting gears feels impossible. Instead of truly resting, the system gravitates toward habits that simulate relief but actually sustain the stress cycle: caffeine to generate false energy, comfort eating to numb, alcohol to disengage, doom-scrolling or binge-watching to avoid stillness, and social withdrawal to minimize stimulation. These aren't moral failings—they're adaptive strategies from a system that believes it cannot afford to downshift.[7]

And this is also why drastic changes backfire. Dieting, jumping into intense exercise, or forcing yourself into rigid self-care routines may seem like "the right things," but to a nervous system running on fumes, they register as added stress. Cortisol spikes. Gut-brain communication disruption. Increased inflammation. The very efforts intended to "get you back on track" leave you feeling even further behind.

This is the hidden driver of the loop: The harder you push, the more stuck you feel. Not because you lack discipline or motivation, but because the underlying imbalance hasn't been addressed.

---

6. Sapolsky, R. M. (2004). Why zebras don't get ulcers: The acclaimed guide to stress, stress-related diseases, and coping. Holt Paperbacks.

7. McEwen, B. S. (2007). Physiology and neurobiology of stress and adaptation: Central role of the brain. Physiological Reviews, 87(3), 873–904. https://doi.org/10.1152/physrev.00041.2006

Delving into the somatic embodiment of your intentions can change your brain. When your body seeks healing, it often recognizes dissatisfaction with its current state but may not know what a better state could be. Gaining clarity about your desired future and allowing yourself to feel what that would be like can open doors to new possibilities.

What shifted things with my client wasn't a better plan—it was addressing the underlying state first. After we did the meditation, we practiced the alchemy techniques from this newfound place of clarity. We crafted SMART goals from a place of success and established her business as a separate energy system.

She began to work with this framework. As a skilled energy healer and meditator, she applied those abilities to her business. However, three months into the program, she reached out to me, distressed. "Shelley," she said, "I'm about to lose my house. The money hasn't come in, and everything has dried up."

She expressed regret about a job offer she had turned down about six weeks earlier. "I didn't want to work for anyone else anymore; I wanted to be my own boss. Now I regret that decision. How much better could I be doing, and how much more could we accomplish together if I had accepted that job?"

I reassured her, "Don't worry. We can put your program on pause, but continue with your daily practice. You've set yourself up for success. You know what you want and have a daily routine in place. Just keep going, and when you're ready, you can come back to me."

Three months later, I received an email from her. "You know what, Shelley? First, I stood firm and said no to that job. Then, a day after our last session, they contacted me again after interviewing other candidates because they couldn't find anyone as qualified as I am."

The fact that we had already analyzed her budget and identified her bottom line allowed her to negotiate a significantly better offer than the initial one. She knew exactly what she needed because we had determined that beforehand. With her baseline established, she decided to let go of all her other clients and contracts. She focused entirely on this one client, which not only covered all her financial bases but also freed up her time for the work she truly enjoyed. Not only that, but she paid off her mortgage and her debts, and for the first time ever, she had $20,000 in the bank.

It was incredible for me to witness this transformation.

What ultimately shifted everything for her wasn't the length of the coaching agreement—it was the steadiness of her daily practice. No amount of willpower or strategy could override the pattern her nervous system had been wired for years to operate on. When stuck in sympathetic overdrive, the nervous system is constantly scanning for danger, even when none is present. This is the same state that drives all-or-nothing thinking—feeling like you must do everything perfectly or not at all—and fuels the impulse to reach for quick fixes. For her, that showed up as overspending on programs, impulsively investing in anything that promised relief, and making decisions from urgency rather than clarity. These weren't personal flaws or failures; they were survival responses from a system trying to soothe itself in the only ways it knew how.

But the daily practice gave her system something it had never truly had: a predictable, regulating rhythm. Each time she engaged with the practice, she signaled to her body that it no longer had to stay hypervigilant. Gradually, her system downshifted out of survival mode. Her cortisol levels normalized. Her thinking became clearer. She could evaluate opportunities without fear flooding her decision-making. She no longer needed constant reassurance from coaching because her body was no longer bracing for impact every moment of the day.

The practice became the stabilizing force that allowed her to reconnect with herself and orient toward her future with a grounded sense of possibility. Daily practice is such a powerful tool for gently retraining the nervous system to exit the overdrive state, making space for calm, discernment, and the capacity to move through life without abandoning yourself.

In another client case, the stuckness did not show up as panic or overspending. It appeared as restraint, austerity, and an unconscious ceiling on success. The shift still began with awareness and daily integration. This client was a wonderful, charismatic person with a deep passion for real estate. He had worked in the real estate market for many years but had never broken the six-figure mark. He joined my year-long coaching program, and for him, it all clicked within the first few weeks. Through our process, he gained clarity on what he truly wanted and why. Working alongside his therapist, he identified an ancestral pattern rooted in his immigrant background. His parents came from a culture that valued austerity and humility and selflessness—yet there he was in the U.S., trying to thrive in real estate, attempting to make sales and close deals. Despite having done personal development work—including programs like Tony Robbins'—he still held onto his ancestors' limiting beliefs. I introduced him to the archetype of the "Prostitute." You may remember that the Prostitute symbolizes how much of our dreams or security we're willing to sacrifice for a sense of stability. I often refer to this archetype when discussing limitations. However, this brilliant client surprised me by expressing the opposite need.

He felt he was too austere in his business dealings and sales calls. He realized that he needed to be more flexible with his values to make the sale. He understood how his ancestral values were interfering with his ability to help people find their dream homes, and he recognized that those values didn't belong in his role as a real estate agent. This was affecting his joy and satisfaction in his job. Remarkably, within a few weeks, he became a millionaire. The work hadn't just changed his thinking; it had restructured the energetic patterns his ambition had been filtered through for years.

My years of training in integrative energy anatomy helped me understand that manifestation is not purely mental—it is structural. The body's energy systems, subtle fields, and vortex centers act like the "software" through which intentions are filtered. When you meditate on the vortex, you are not visualizing in the abstract. You are engaging the exact energy architecture that reorganizes your reality from the inside out.

Tara Swart's Neuroscience-Based View of Manifestation

Neuroscientist and leadership adviser Tara Swart reframes manifestation not as magical thinking but as a neurobiological process through which intention, attention, and action reshape the brain's internal landscape. In her model, desired outcomes emerge when we align emotionally resonant goals with the brain's capacity for neuroplastic change. Manifestation becomes a disciplined practice of priming the brain to recognize opportunities, take purposeful risks, and reinforce behaviors that support long-term transformation.

At the center of Swart's work are two mechanisms that explain why visualization and intention-setting can influence real-world outcomes. The first is selective attention—the brain's filtering system that determines which stimuli reach conscious awareness. By repeatedly focusing on a goal, the brain becomes more likely to notice information and opportunities that support it.[8] The second is value tagging, a process by which emotionally significant images and ideas are marked as high-priority in the limbic system. When a goal is infused with meaning, the brain allocates more cognitive resources to pursuing it, creating a bias toward action.[9]

Swart also emphasizes that manifestation is far more effective when the goal is what she calls a magnetic desire—a deeply aligned, emotionally charged intention. These desires mobilize motivation circuits, stabilize focus, and reduce internal resistance. In this sense, manifestation becomes less about forcing an outcome and more about creating inner coherence between purpose, emotion, and behavior.

An abundance mindset, another pillar of her model, shifts the brain from the threat-based vigilance of scarcity into a more expansive state. Research on cognitive broadening shows that positive affect increases creativity, flexibility, and risk tolerance—capacities essential for entrepreneurship and leadership.[10] This mindset opens the perceptual field instead of contracting it.

Finally, the entire process is held together by neuroplasticity. Repetition of thought, imagery, and action strengthens neural pathways, while new behaviors gradually override old patterns.[11] Swart's approach mirrors the distinction between manifestation and alchemy: manifestation names the outcome, while neuroplasticity is one mechanism through which the inner transformation becomes possible.

Practical Application

Swart recommends a structured approach for bringing intentions into form:

---

8. Broadbent, D. E. (1958). Perception and communication. Pergamon Press. Corbetta, M., & Shulman, G. L. (2002). Control of goal-directed and stimulus-driven attention in the brain. Nature Reviews Neuroscience, 3(3), 201–215.https://doi.org/10.1038/nrn755

9. Swart, T. (2018). The source: Open your mind, change your life. HarperCollins.

10. Fredrickson, "The Role of Positive Emotions."

11. Pascual-Leone, A., Amedi, A., Fregni, F., & Merabet, L. B. (2005). The plastic human brain cortex. Annual Review of Neuroscience, 28, 377–401. https://doi.org/10.1146/annurev.neuro.27.070203.144216

- Clarify the "why." Define the deeper purpose behind a goal and align it with personal values. Journaling enhances self-awareness and strengthens prefrontal engagement.

- Visualize consistently. Vivid mental imagery stimulates many of the same neural circuits used in action, priming the brain to pursue the goal.

- Use affirmations and gratitude practices. Positive self-referential statements and gratitude activate dopaminergic reward pathways, reinforcing motivation and self-worth.[12]

- Translate vision into behavior. Swart warns against passive dreaming; action boards and concrete steps convert intention into embodied practice.

- Practice patience and persistence. Neural change is incremental. Self-compassion sustains the process and prevents threat-based collapse.

In this view, manifestation is less about controlling outcomes and more about shaping the internal conditions that make aligned outcomes more available. It reflects a partnership between purpose, perception, and the brain's innate capacity to reorganize itself around what matters most.

---

12. Househam, A. M., Peterson, C. T., Mills, P. J., & Chopra, D. (2017). The effects of a gratitude intervention on mental well-being: A systematic review. Journal of Alternative and Complementary Medicine, 23(11), 803–811. https://doi.org/10.1089/acm.2017.0050

Chapter Ten

Becoming Home

I arrived at a profound period of completion in my life. For the first time, the many threads of my personal work, professional training, and business development were converging. Receiving my master's degree in coaching with a health and peak performance coaching certificate was a major milestone that integrated years of inner work. The disruptions and repeating cycles that once defined my path finally began to settle. What once felt chaotic revealed itself as a long-awaited closing of loops.

From July 2022 through July 2023, I was devoted to wedding planning. My husband and I navigated having a ceremony in New York City during COVID and working with the restrictions that came with it. It was quite an adventure. At the same time, we put his apartment on the market, found a new place we loved, and started the process of selling our current apartment while renovating the new one we'd purchased. In July, we got married.

In September, I took my exam to become an ICF Professional Certified Coach and passed. It felt like a rite of passage, opening the door for me to fulfill my dream of offering an ICF-accredited program. This would enable me to share my tools in an evidence-based and ethical way while connecting people with the global community of coaches supported by this respected professional organization. With all of these accomplishments bolstering me, I finally had the capacity to address a long-standing feeling of incompleteness.

During this whirlwind of personal life changes, my existing program began to decline. The old ways weren't working like they used to. I remember a pivotal moment in the fall of 2022 during a coaching call with my mastermind group—those who had for years gone through my meditation certification, Reiki training, and business alchemy studies. It was a close-knit and intimate group.

As we were wrapping up our year-long immersion program, someone asked about the value of daily practice. During this discussion, it became clear that many in the group weren't utilizing the daily practice at all. I explained how daily practice serves as a keystone for overcoming obstacles. It's about showing up every day and facing the challenges linked to what you want to create. This process addresses everything that changes your relationship to your goals. It builds new neurological pathways associated with success while helping the pathways associated with old habits fade away.

Then, one person chimed in, recalling a moment from a couple of years prior when someone was struggling to complete a 30-day practice. I had suggested she attempt a 90-day practice instead, and everyone laughed, finding it absurd. If she couldn't manage 30 days, how could she possibly do 90?

At that moment, I realized that this close group of people was missing something crucial. This explained why they were still with me, grappling with certain issues and feeling stuck despite our time together. We had a significant misunderstanding. I wasn't suggesting they practice every day for 90 days. What I meant was that if they couldn't make it through 30 days, they needed to keep practicing and not give up.

The point of the practice is that if you miss a day, or life gets busy and you haven't done your daily practice for a week, just return to it. Give yourself 90 days to complete those 30 days. Sometimes, the changes we are trying to make are so substantial that our whole nervous system feels overwhelmed, or life interferes despite our best intentions. This is often the moment when we give up, thinking, *This just doesn't work for me.* The key is to keep going.

Eventually, you will make it through 30 whole days, and it will get easier. The more you practice, the easier it becomes. I now do 100-day practices. The first time I did one was the hardest thing I've ever experienced. It took me more than 100 days to finish it.

Now, I love the experience. Every hundred days, I change my intention, and it has become an integral part of my BizAttune process. I believe this practice has been crucial in helping me address those "scratches on a record" patterns very effectively. A scratch on a record causes a needle to skip every time it reaches that point. The same goes for our aimless habits. Committing to a 100-day practice allows me to smooth out the grooves and build habits that flow and are aligned with my life.

The misunderstanding with my group gave everyone a good laugh at my expense and helped me wrap up my master's program with gratitude. The momentum that had helped me accumulate all those hours and deepen my practice shifted and reached its limits. I revamped everything into a different format for the next group that would be called to work with me.

Many in the existing group felt it was time to work independently, acknowledging that they had been using me as a crutch—a realization I fully supported. It's a proud moment when the people you mentor can move forward with the tools to work independently. It has been wonderful to see how they have embraced the BizAttune process and developed their own relationship with it. Even a year or two after that program ended, their desired results are still unfolding.

When things don't happen immediately, we tend to interpret that as a sign that it's not meant to be. In reality, it's often just a matter of maintaining that daily practice and gradually chipping away at the obstacles. Sometimes, the challenges are deeply ingrained, as I experienced with the many layers I had to unpack before I could find space for myself.

As I worked to reshape my program, everything seemed to come together as I reached a deeper understanding of my relationship to the BizAttune process. I realized that I had invested so much into helping others master this tool. I dedicated significant time to research so I could teach it in a meaningful and relevant way, regardless of people's backgrounds or their beliefs about energy.

After completing my degree and essentially "graduating" my year-long group of clients, I understood that I needed to spend some time focusing on my own journey while engaging a little less with the outside world. I was married, we had moved into our newly renovated apartment, and we were in the process of settling in.

I began integrating coaching tools more intentionally into my process, including evidence-based assessments such as the Wheel of Life and the VIA Character Strengths Survey.

The Wheel of Life, a coaching framework developed by Paul J. Meyer in the 1960s, offered a clear visual snapshot of satisfaction across key dimensions—career, finances, health, relationships, personal growth, recreation, family, spirituality, and community. By placing these areas side by side, it made patterns visible that were otherwise easy to overlook, revealing where my energy was concentrated and where I was neglecting myself. I had always leaned toward spiritual growth, but the wheel highlighted imbalances I could no longer ignore.

What stood out most was how low my professional relationship satisfaction appeared during a major life transition. As relationships shifted, I started releasing people-pleasing patterns and prioritizing connections that felt mutually supportive and aligned with my values. The Wheel of Life became more than a reflective exercise;[1] it functioned as a perceptual tool, helping me recognize where nurturing was needed and where boundaries were essential.[2]

I integrated my spiritual tools—sacred geometry and archetypes—to clarify intentions and embody the qualities I wanted in relationships. I called in my energetic board of advisors, such as Shahida Arabi, whose work on relational dynamics helped me recognize how overgiving had distorted my sense of connection. The wheel became a practical way to track these relational shifts.

Over time, I aligned each life dimension with specific archetypal qualities and role models. This blending of structured assessment and spiritual reflection evolved into a client practice, helping them map support systems, clarify resources, and approach growth more intentionally.

As my work with the positive shadow deepened, I sought tools that could identify strengths clients overlooked. The VIA Character Strengths Survey, developed by Peterson and Seligman as part of the positive psychology movement, became a natural complement.[3] This research-based assessment highlights 24 universal strengths.

---

1. Meyer, P. J. (1960). Success Motivation Institute materials.

2. Whitworth, L., Kimsey-House, H., Kimsey-House, K., & Sandahl, P. (2007). Co-Active coaching: New skills for coaching people toward success in work and life. Davies-Black Publishing.

3. Peterson, C., & Seligman, M. E. P. (2004). Character strengths and virtues: A handbook and classification. Oxford University Press.

Clients often recognize their top strengths immediately; these become anchors during change. More revealing, however, are underutilized strengths—qualities not absent, but underdeveloped. These often mirror the positive shadow: capacities that feel unfamiliar yet are essential for growth.

Research supports this approach. Strengths such as hope, optimism, and love correlate with stronger relationships and higher well-being. Studies during the COVID-19 lockdown found that using those specific character strengths, regardless of them being a personal top strength, predicted improvements in mental health over time.[4] Activating strengths, especially during stress or transition, increases stability and engagement.

The VIA framework gives language to qualities clients may not have claimed as their own. Growth becomes less about becoming someone new and more about activating what was already present. In this way, structured strengths work becomes an evidence-informed extension of positive shadow integration.

Then, the dean of my master's program called to inform me that she would be stepping away from the program. The position of lead faculty was opening up, and she stated that I was the only person she thought of for the role. A bolt of excitement went through me. I had an intuitive sense from the beginning of my master's program that the school would hire me one day. It was an entirely unfounded vision, and now it was happening.

She had always been a positive, reassuring, and supportive mentor to me. She said, "I didn't think of anyone else. I know your dream is to have your own certification program, and this opportunity will help you with that. You will gain real-life experience teaching as a faculty member within an ICF-accredited program, which will further assist in the development of your own program."

I accepted the position, where I taught Business Skills for Coaches and served as lead faculty for a year. I knew going in that it wouldn't be a long-term opportunity, as the new president was phasing out the Master's of Health and Human Performance and Health Coaching certification programs. Interestingly, I viewed this as a synchronicity. It felt like

4. Martínez-Martí, M. L., Avia, M. D., & Hernández-Lloreda, M. J. (2020).The effects of character strengths on well-being during the COVID-19 pandemic: Evidence from Spain. Frontiers in Psychology, 11, 566943.https://doi.org/10.3389/fpsyg.2020.566943

kismet: I could teach temporarily as part of my training, then make a graceful transition as I developed my own offering. I felt incredibly supported throughout this journey.

My orientation toward change had been shaped years earlier by a small book called *The Dance of Becoming*. Along with titles like *Attitude Is Everything*, it shaped how I thought about growth and change.

Written by Stuart Heller, the book is a series of short meditations—sometimes just a single word on a page. The practice is simple: read one page a day and let it settle without trying to analyze or master it.

Heller had been a professional dancer who studied martial arts and yoga before becoming an executive coach. I found his emphasis on "becoming" in my early twenties, and his path of integrating movement, discipline, and leadership resonated deeply with my own.

He outlined a five-step progression: I got it. I remember it. I use it. I know it. I am it.

"I got it" feels like completion, but it is only the start. Insight alone doesn't transform us. We often understand something, forget it, and return to the beginning. The shift happens at "I use it." Practice turns understanding into embodiment. Becoming unfolds through repetition, lived experience, and time.

The journey of embodiment has been pivotal for me. I saw how my vortex had been guiding me toward awareness of how little I was fully allowing myself to receive and enjoy the opportunities and gifts in my life. This pattern traced back to childhood, where I internalized the belief that wanting things for myself—whether health, time, creative expression, or even a home—was selfish or excessive. I learned to prioritize helping and serving others, often at the expense of my own desires. Over time, this led me to unconsciously resist or deflect opportunities, making it difficult for them to take root fully.

Through this process, I developed a new relationship with ownership. Working with the vortex showed me that becoming the person I'm meant to be requires allowing myself to have something—to claim desires instead of holding them at a distance. I learned to take ownership of both the BizAttune process and the identity that emerges from it, and that ownership became the foundation for deep and lasting transformation.

It shifted my focus from striving toward outcomes to actually inhabiting the path itself. Instead of treating goals as proof of worth or validation, I experienced them as expressions of who I was becoming. For the first time, I allowed myself to want something for myself, to set goals without apology, and to recognize that what I create along the way is already enough.

The outdated mindset of competition I carried unconsciously was never something I acknowledged intellectually. I'd been conditioned to believe that if I shone, I was somehow taking away from someone else. However, the BizAttune process helped me understand that shining does not diminish others; instead, it invites them to shine as well. The tools I've developed and the support I've received have allowed me to inhabit this space much more fully.

Over time, the practices that guided my own transformation evolved into a structured process I could teach.

Thanks to this journey, I love helping others discover their potential. I recognize the same subconscious patterns within others, and supporting them as they face challenges they didn't believe they could overcome and uncover powers they didn't know they had is a joy. It inspires me to show up every single day. What began as personal experimentation gradually evolved into a structured process that others could apply in their own lives and businesses.

The BizAttune Business Vortex Framework

This process begins with the understanding that sustainable manifestation is not about forcing change but about gently reorganizing energy, attention, and behavior over time in a way that can be sustained. Rather than driving change through effort alone, it emphasizes a sense of stability and the system's capacity to adapt, allowing new patterns to take hold.

While traditional thirty-day habit practices focus on adding a nourishing behavior and removing a depleting one to rewire neural pathways, this method goes deeper. It integrates intention, embodied awareness, and daily feedback loops to create alignment before acceleration.

At its foundation is crafting a clear, emotionally resonant intention, paired with structured daily practices that free up energetic bandwidth and redirect it toward a desired outcome. As old neural and behavioral patterns lose momentum, new pathways are strengthened through repetition, embodied focus, and intentional reinforcement.

Rather than relying on willpower alone, this approach creates a dynamic, self-organizing structure that supports intuitive calibration. Participants develop an ongoing reflective relationship with their intention, learning to read signals, refine direction, and respond to feedback in real time. The BizAttune process becomes living and adaptive rather than rigid and outcome-obsessed.

The methodology acknowledges that misalignment, timing, health, skill development, or unconscious limitations may surface during expansion. Instead of treating obstacles as failures, they are approached as informative data that strengthens long-term sustainability. Progress unfolds in cycles of growth, recalibration, and integration.

Celebration and integration are built into the framework. Success is consciously embodied and stabilized before moving forward, preventing the common pattern of achievement followed by regression.

Step 1: Clarify the Target

Begin with a clear, affirmative intention that includes both the desired outcome and the felt experience of living it. This becomes your directional focus. The aim is not merely achievement, but alignment with something that is genuinely right for you.

Step 2: Reclaim Bandwidth

Add one nourishing daily behavior and remove one depleting daily behavior for thirty days. When an old pattern is no longer reinforced, its neural network begins to weaken. The energy and attention it once consumed become available to support the new pathway you are building.

Step 3: Embody the Desire

Rather than holding the intention as an abstract goal, engage it somatically. Spend time each day experiencing it in the body and nervous system. This stabilizes the emotional and physiological state that supports the outcome.

Step 4: Establish Support Structures

Consciously choose the internal and external influences that will reinforce your new direction. This may include mentors, peers, practices, or environments that stabilize coherence and reduce interference.

Step 5: Broadcast Through Action

Each day, take small, aligned steps from the identity of someone already living the outcome. Ask yourself what actions reflected that reality. This shifts attention from chasing results to embodying them.

Step 6: Use Results as Feedback

Approach every outcome with curiosity. Wins, delays, disappointments, and surprises are all information. Instead of forcing change, refine your approach based on what reality reflects back to you. This is self-study grounded in working with things as they are.

Step 7: Work the Mirror

When something feels stuck externally, investigate internally. Outer obstacles often reflect beliefs, limitations, skill gaps, or energetic contractions that are ready to be addressed. Expansion may require strengthening health, building capacity, or releasing self-imposed ceilings.

Step 8: Normalize the Cycles

Growth is not linear. Periods of momentum may be followed by recalibration. Health priorities, skill development, and identity shifts are not detours but part of building sustainable success. Trust deepens as the pattern of support becomes visible over time.

Step 9: Celebrate and Integrate

Acknowledge every aligned step. Celebration stabilizes new neural pathways and reinforces coherence. Sometimes the win is tangible. Sometimes it is resilience, awareness, or grace under pressure. No acknowledgment is too small.

Step 10: Continue the Evolution

Completion of a cycle is not an endpoint but an integration phase. Before setting a new target, allow space to consolidate gains, recalibrate identity, and fully embody the transformation.

In essence, this is not simply a habit challenge. It is an embodied alchemical process that blends neuroscience, behavior design, intuitive development, and structured reflection to produce coherent, sustainable outcomes. It trains individuals to work strategically with their energy and attention so that manifestation becomes less about force and more about alignment, refinement, and long-term integration.

The Framework in Practice

My client, Celeste, was one of the first people I worked with to implement business alchemy—and one of the biggest success stories to emerge from it. She was a fitness professional who came to me at a breaking point. She was a poster child for the industry: teaching group fitness classes in and around New York City, coaching multiple private clients, exercising two to three hours a day, dieting, cleansing, and keeping a relentless schedule. Her income reflected the instability of the fitness industry: low five figures, dependent on an unsustainable volume of work, and often simply grateful for opportunities to gain exposure through unpaid work as a dancer or in minor acting roles. She looked like the rising artist in New York—disciplined, committed, doing everything right, with a bright future ahead. But her body told a different story: she was exhausted.

At the same time, another tension was shaping her life. Celeste had long dreamed of becoming an actress, but the structure of her career made it almost impossible to pursue that path. Her fitness work, her health priorities, her training regimen, her auditions, and her financial well-being were all pulling in different directions. Time spent teaching or coaching meant missing auditions. Time spent preparing for auditions meant losing income. The effort required to maintain her physique often came at the expense of her energy levels. Everything existed in competition. One priority was always sacrificed for another.

Despite her best efforts, Celeste's symptoms kept worsening: disrupted sleep, mood swings, hormonal imbalance, digestive distress, inflammation, and constant overwhelm. She had a predisposition toward autoimmune issues from childhood illness, and the combination of overtraining, undernourishment, and nonstop stress was pushing her system into deeper dysregulation. Her refrain became, "I'm doing all the right things, and everything is getting worse."

A functional medicine evaluation confirmed what her body had been saying all along: the strategies meant to keep her "healthy" were actually overwhelming her nervous system. The lifestyle required to maintain her career was incompatible with her physiology.

This became the pivot point. Instead of pouring more energy into hustle-based fitness norms, we explored a different question: How could her health, body, career goals, and lifelong dreams work together? Rather than treating each part of her life as a separate problem to solve, we began looking at how these elements could function as one system.

Using the BizAttune process, we reframed the situation. Instead of asking which priority should win—health, income, auditions, or career stability—we asked how each element could support the others.

With that clarity, Celeste redirected her strategy. Instead of working harder, she worked more strategically—targeting opportunities that aligned with her values, energy needs, and desired lifestyle.

One of those opportunities was a high-profile fitness contract that transformed the entire equation. Instead of continuing to piece together unstable income from multiple classes and clients, she secured a multi-year agreement that moved her from low five-figure earnings into well above six figures. The contract included a stable salary, benefits, a wellness stipend, and free clothing, reducing her expenses while creating a predictable schedule that supported her health.

That stability created space she had never had before. When auditions came in unexpectedly, she now had the time and bandwidth to pursue them. The visibility of the contract also elevated her personal brand, expanding her professional portfolio and creating commercial opportunities that supported her acting career. What had once been competing priorities reinforced each other. Her fitness work supported financial stability. Financial stability supported her health. Her health supported her creative capacity. And the visibility of her work strengthened her acting career.

As Celeste's nervous system stabilized, her symptoms began to resolve. Her bandwidth expanded. She started thriving again—creatively, personally, and physically. With better health and a career structure that supported her, she finally had the capacity to focus on other areas of life that mattered to her: partnerships, community, and artistic work. She landed high-profile paid acting jobs, stabilized her health, and eventually met her partner and got married.

At one point, she returned for a three-month "tune-up" program with me, just before her contract was up for renegotiation. The company planned to significantly reduce her compensation despite her strong performance. This news couldn't have come at a worse time.

She had recently gotten married, so she was paying off the wedding costs, moving into a new apartment, and trying to start a family. In our work together, we took the laundry list of things that needed to get done and strategized ways to do it efficiently. We looked at a strategic and achievable payoff plan for the wedding, ways to move at low or no cost, and lifestyle interventions that allowed her to keep her health a priority while also refining her negotiation strategy. We worked on strengthening her boundaries and anchored her in the value she brought to the organization.

Rather than approaching these challenges as isolated problems, we looked at how each decision could support the others—financial planning, housing, health, and career negotiations—working together rather than competing for attention.

As a result, she not only preserved her original contract rate; she also secured an additional two years under the same high-value terms she had previously earned while successfully moving, paying off her debt, and becoming pregnant.

We helped determine where she wanted to be and identified how everything was working together, including her daily practice. Celeste's breakthrough came when she stopped trying to follow industry norms and instead aligned her lifestyle with the intelligence of her own body and long-term vision.

What had once felt like an impossible balancing act—health, finances, fitness, and acting—became an integrated system in which each element strengthened the others.

Celeste's experience illustrates the central principle of the BizAttune framework: when health, career, finances, and personal aspirations are treated as parts of a single system rather than competing priorities, strategic decisions can simultaneously advance multiple goals.

Chapter Eleven

Turning Goals Into Presence

I have encountered the power of daily practice through many lenses. I've explored the Taoist approach, Tantric philosophy, positive psychology, and neuroscience. Each offers valuable insights. Yet emerging research suggests something surprisingly simple: the specific practice may matter less than the act of committing to something consistently each day.[1] The repetition itself strengthens neuroplasticity, gradually rewiring the brain for change.

If daily practice is already reshaping the brain's capacity for adaptation, it raises an important question: why not choose a practice specifically designed to improve how we lead, decide, and perform in business?

This commitment does something deeper than improve discipline or build a habit. Daily practice trains the body and nervous system to process information in a more organized way. When the business is treated as its own energetic system rather than something the body must carry inside the nervous system, the two systems begin to coordinate with one another. Attention, energy, and resources start organizing around what you are building. Information relevant to your goals, opportunities, and decisions begins to surface more

---

1. Lally, P., van Jaarsveld, C. H. M., Potts, H. W. W., & Wardle, J. (2010). How are habits formed: Modeling habit formation in the real world. *European Journal of Social Psychology, 40*(6), 998–1009. https://doi.org/10.1002/ejsp.674

clearly. This alignment strengthens pattern recognition, insight, and discernment—the foundation for developing and strengthening business intuition.

This commitment changes the brain. It can be as straightforward as engaging in an activity every day, or it can involve creating more structured protocols, similar to the framework I implement in my business alchemy work.

I work with many high-achieving, high-performing individuals who check all the typical boxes that define success—the milestones, the accomplishments, the external markers of achievement. They are doing everything they were taught to do, yet many still don't feel successful. Something is missing.

In my experience, that missing element is rarely another strategy or productivity system. More often, it is the absence of a daily practice that reconnects the body, mind, and business.

Through meditation and embodiment practices that create energetic separation between the entrepreneur and the business itself, people begin to access something different: greater clarity, a steadier nervous system, and the intuitive insight needed to make better decisions and avoid costly mistakes.[2]

I've come to see daily practice as the keystone. In architecture, a keystone is the critical piece that holds everything together, creating a self-supporting and self-sustaining structure. In much the same way, daily practice becomes the element that allows the body, mind, and business to organize around sustainable success.

Over time, this practice becomes the foundation for sustainable performance—allowing the business to grow without the overwhelm that so often accompanies success.

This process helps unpack the habitual patterns of overworking and overdoing, shifting focus from those extrinsic measures of success to tapping into intrinsic measures based on

---

2. Robinson, Bryan. "Meditation Reduces Mind Wandering and Mistakes at Work, New Studies Show." *Forbes*, April 4, 2022.https://www.forbes.com/sites/bryanrobinson/2022/04/04/meditation-reduces-mind-wandering-and-mistakes-at-work-new-studies-show/ https://www.forbes.com/sites/bryanrobinson/2022/04/04/meditation-reduces-mind-wandering-and-mistakes-at-work-new-studies-show/ .

values and beliefs. Once you understand the value behind your goals, you might find that what you thought you wanted isn't what you truly desire, allowing you to redefine your extrinsic measures of success. When you know what you want—your "why"—you can make decisions in the moment with clarity. This understanding brings a sense of freedom from the constraints that limit not only what you can achieve but also how you envision what is possible. When you know why you're doing what you're doing, you can relate to everything you experience from a place of possibility.

In positive psychology, there's a concept called affective forecasting, which refers to our tendency to misjudge how future events will affect our emotions. We often overestimate how happy good things will make us, and how difficult challenges will feel, which means we're not always accurate in predicting what will actually bring us fulfillment.

When pursuing the idea of success or envisioning where we want to be, it's easy to orient toward an expected emotional outcome. We work hard to get there, only to find that the experience doesn't match what we imagined. In this way, goals are often shaped by assumption rather than alignment. The BizAttune process helps unpack that misconception.

As that shift occurs, the question itself begins to change. It's no longer, "How do I use the opportunities, experiences, and results that are arising to get to where I know I want to be?" But rather, "How do I use the opportunities, experiences, and results that are arising to stay aligned with what I know matters—even when they don't look the way I expected?"

I had a client who was only motivated by debt. Whenever she tried to save, she'd end up spending it and falling deeper into debt instead. So we worked with that tendency rather than against it—using good debt to grow her business and structuring her finances so she could save and invest while still carrying debt. Over time, she built habits that no longer relied on it. By accessing that feeling, new possibilities began to emerge.

We are training our nervous systems to recognize what that feeling state is and to make decisions from a place of flow and coherence instead of effort. Through my experience, I've learned there isn't one "right" way to manifest. I've often done the opposite of what business coaches and typical manifestation practices suggest. At various stages of my journey, I chose to go against conventional wisdom and used my intuition to discover what truly worked for me.

What worked for me might not work for you. Each of us has a unique manifesting blueprint, and true manifestation guides us toward our personal peak performance—our personal best. This state isn't created by chasing external outcomes. It emerges when we learn to embody the feeling of fulfillment in the present.

Treating your business as a separate energy system can coach you toward sustainable outcomes and help you access your personal peak performance. Many people who have gone through this process have told me that they often forgot their original goals. They became so immersed in being present and enjoying the BizAttune process that their initial ambitions faded into the background. I like to say we transform goals into presence. When you create from a state of presence, anything becomes possible.

We learn to step out of our own way and let go of rigid ideas about what we want to create. In this space, anything can happen at any moment. We move away from the habit of striving and instead embrace simply being in our lives. It's natural to desire what you think will make you happy. That's completely valid. We start from that place and use this process to unpack those desires.

The key is understanding that feeling stuck does not mean we aren't meant to achieve our desires. It's a common experience that arises when we confront the dense habits and patterns from our past. As we move forward, we need to unpack and break through these dense energies, redirecting that momentum toward our goals. Establishing a daily practice provides a sustainable way to gradually face those challenges, tackling them piece by piece.

Rather than striving endlessly toward a goal, we learn to access flow states to meet the daily challenges that arise. In this way, we can respond to life's events without succumbing to stress and overwhelm. If you find it difficult to maintain consistency with a 30-day practice, as my wonderful coaching group did, give yourself more time. It's okay to miss a day or even a week; life happens. What matters is returning to your daily practice. Over time, it's not about checking off a box for daily completion, but rather what that consistency cultivates: a repurposing and restructuring of your foundations to support and align with sustainable success.

Can you achieve a breakthrough without daily practice? Absolutely. Can you make progress in your business without treating it as a separate energy system? Of course. People do it all the time. I have found that adding a BizAttune practice can make the process easier.

When we begin to unpack the energetics of a business, many of us over-identify with it, saying, "I am my business." But the body is already processing an enormous amount of information at any given moment. When the business becomes fused with that system, it adds another layer of pressure.

What we are doing here is optimizing efficiency by applying the neuroscience of change, the principles of alchemy and manifestation, and the business vortex model—rather than carrying the stress of the business inside the body. Some of my clients have asked me if this approach is considered cheating since it takes away the "working hard to prove your value" aspect of professional life. Not at all! In Taoist alchemical philosophy, the idea is to apply effort in the most efficient way to achieve the best outcome—that is the essence of alchemy.

One of the fastest ways to reduce overwhelm is to stop carrying your business inside your nervous system. When we separate the two—treating the business as its own energy system—we free the body to process experience more easily while the business develops its own momentum.

This way, you create two energy systems that are aligned and coherent, working toward the same goal, which ultimately makes everything easier. Clarity of intention and readiness for change are crucial components in this process. Your daily practice helps you gradually prepare, ensuring that nothing feels too overwhelming or leads to significant setbacks. Taking small steps is essential.

This over-identification comes with a cost. When you overly identify with your business, you tend to process both personal and business-related information simultaneously. If you rely solely on extrinsic measures of success while checking items off a list, you become entrenched in the business world, which is centered around constant doing and achieving. This can lead to your nervous system being locked in sympathetic overdrive.

This is where daily practice becomes essential. Daily practice is not simply a wellness routine. It is the mechanism that restores the physiological flexibility required for creativity, intuition, and effective decision-making.

In this state, the nervous system operates on perfectionism, hypervigilance, and relentless pushing. These patterns limit our access to alternative ways of being. Our bodies can become overwhelmed, making it difficult to shift out of sympathetic overdrive, since maintaining that state requires so much energy. We can inherit these patterns from our ancestors, or we may be born predisposed to sympathetic overdrive. Consequently, when we enter environments that push us, we may not even realize there is another way to live.

Over time, I realized something important. Many entrepreneurs believe they are stuck because they lack strategy or discipline. In reality, they are often overwhelmed because their nervous system, identity, and business have become intertwined. When those systems are fused, every challenge in the business can feel like a personal threat. Daily practice creates the separation needed for clarity. Once the body has space to process experience, the business can evolve without overwhelming the person running it.

What I discovered is the importance of separating your business and career, treating them as distinct energy systems.

This allows us to clarify intentions, embody the feeling of success, and help your brain and nervous system recalibrate to a different emotional state. When your business gets its own lungs and heart, your body can stop over-breathing for everyone else. Separation creates coherence; coherence creates capacity—for family, prosperity, and the creative life you're here to live.

As this process unfolds, our daily practice plays a crucial role in supporting unwinding and integration, one step at a time. Peak performance is not created by pushing harder. It emerges when the systems that shape our lives—body, mind, and work—begin to move in the same direction.

When you're in sympathetic overdrive, even minor changes can reset your system. In a state of overwhelm, you might feel the urge to completely overhaul your life, such as sell your business, fire all your clients, and start fresh. You might want to join a fitness boot camp and revamp your diet all at once or go cold turkey on coffee. However, when your nervous system is already taxed, any change—small or large—can disrupt the fragile balance of your system. Therefore, readiness for change is vital when it comes to repatterning these behaviors, and a consistent daily practice provides significant support in that process.

Over time, you begin to shift from striving toward goals in ways that inadvertently work against them to allowing your business to guide you toward presence, where unexpected insights and outcomes arise with greater ease and enjoyment.

The Physiology of Sympathetic Overdrive: What Heart Rate Variability Reveals

One of the most useful physiological markers for understanding overwhelm is heart rate variability (HRV). Although the term can sound technical, the underlying concept is straightforward. HRV refers to the variation in time between successive heartbeats, known as inter-beat intervals. Rather than beating with perfect mechanical regularity, a healthy heart continually speeds up and slows down in response to internal and external conditions. This variability reflects the body's capacity to adapt to changing demands.

Higher HRV is generally associated with greater physiological resilience, while lower HRV is linked with chronic stress, illness, and reduced capacity for recovery.[3] In essence, HRV reflects how effectively the nervous system can activate during a challenge and then return to baseline once the challenge has passed. Researchers often describe this as autonomic flexibility—the ability of the nervous system to shift efficiently between states of activation and restoration.[4]

At the physiological level, HRV reflects the dynamic interaction between the sympathetic nervous system, which mobilizes the body during stress or exertion, and the parasympathetic nervous system, particularly vagal activity, which supports recovery, digestion, and restoration.[5] When the nervous system is well regulated, these systems operate in a flexible rhythm. When chronic stress accumulates, this flexibility decreases and HRV tends to decline.[6]

---

3. Pham, T., Lau, Z. J., Chen, S. H. A., & Makowski, D. (2021). Heart rate variability in psychology: A review of HRV indices and analysis methods. Sensors, 21(12), 3998. Shaffer, F., & Ginsberg, J. (2017). An overview of heart rate variability metrics and norms. Frontiers in Public Health, 5, 258.

4. Shaffer, F., & Ginsberg, J. (2017). An overview of heart rate variability metrics and norms. Frontiers in Public Health, 5, 258.

5. Thayer, J. F., Åhs, F., Fredrikson, M., Sollers, J., & Wager, T. (2012). A meta-analysis of heart rate variability and neuroimaging studies. Neuroscience & Biobehavioral Reviews, 36(2), 747–756.

6. Kim, H.-G., Cheon, E.-J., Bai, D.-S., Lee, Y.-H., & Koo, B.-H. (2018). Stress and heart rate variability: A meta-analysis and review of the literature. Psychiatry Investigation, 15(3), 235–245.

Understanding HRV also opens a broader perspective on the role of the heart in systemic regulation. In Traditional Chinese Medicine, the heart is described as the "emperor" of the organs, reflecting its role in governing circulation, consciousness, and the integration of bodily processes. Classical texts describe the heart as the seat of Shen, the organizing principle of awareness and vitality within the body.[7] While modern physiology uses different terminology, the idea that the heart plays a central coordinating role within the organism is not entirely foreign to contemporary research.

From a biomedical perspective, the heart and brain operate in a bidirectional regulatory network connected through the autonomic nervous system and the vagus nerve. Signals constantly travel between cardiovascular, respiratory, endocrine, and neural systems to maintain homeostasis.

The heart also generates the strongest measurable rhythmic electrical signal in the human body. Research associated with the HeartMath Institute has reported that the electrical activity recorded from the heart is substantially larger than brain-wave signals measured by EEG and that the magnetic component of this signal can be detected several feet away from the body using sensitive magnetometers. Some researchers have proposed that this field may contribute to whole-system synchronization, although the broader functional implications of these measurements remain an area of ongoing investigation.[8]

Regardless of how one interprets these findings, the physiological relationship between the heart and nervous system plays a critical role in the experience of overwhelm.

When the nervous system is functioning well, the body can rapidly mobilize during challenges and then return efficiently to baseline. This capacity for flexible activation and recovery is reflected in higher HRV.

Chronic stress changes this pattern.

As stress accumulates, the nervous system can shift toward sympathetic dominance, reducing vagal regulation and lowering HRV. In this state the body becomes more easily

---

7. Lv, W., et al. (2021). Understanding traditional Chinese medicine: Integration of traditional and modern perspectives. Frontiers in Pharmacology, 12, 761741.

8. McCraty, R. (2015). The energetic heart: Bioelectromagnetic communication within and between people. Global Advances in Health and Medicine, 4(Suppl), 28–37.

activated and slower to recover. Sleep may be disrupted, digestion impaired, and the mind can enter persistent loops of problem-solving and threat monitoring.

In other words, the system loses flexibility.

Low HRV does not mean the heart cannot increase its rate when needed. The body can still mount a stress response. What changes is the capacity to recover once the stressor has passed. The nervous system becomes slower to settle, and physiological activation can linger long after the original stimulus has disappeared.

An everyday example illustrates the difference.

Imagine stepping into a crosswalk and suddenly noticing a car approaching faster than expected. The body's fight-or-flight response activates instantly. Adrenaline rises, heart rate increases, and you move quickly to safety.

In a well-regulated nervous system, once the danger has passed, the body recalibrates within minutes. Breathing slows, heart rate stabilizes, and attention returns to the present moment.

When HRV is low, the reaction can linger. Hours later, the body may still feel activated. Sleep may be disrupted, and the mind may continue circling the event. The stress response continues long after the situation itself has ended.

This is not a failure of discipline or mindset. It reflects a physiological constraint within the regulatory systems of the body.

From the perspective of sustainable performance, HRV offers an important insight: overwhelm is rarely solved by pushing harder. More often, it resolves when the body regains its ability to mobilize, adapt, and recover.

Practices that strengthen parasympathetic regulation—such as slow breathing, meditation, movement, social connection, and positive emotional states like gratitude—have all been shown to improve HRV and support nervous system flexibility.

Over time, this restored flexibility allows the heart and nervous system to return to their natural rhythm: activation when needed, recovery when possible, and resilience in the face of uncertainty.

The significance of heart rate variability extends beyond stress physiology. As discussed earlier in this book, decision-making is not purely cognitive. The brain continuously integrates signals from the body through interoceptive pathways that communicate information about internal physiological states.

When the nervous system is regulated and autonomic flexibility is high, these signals support emotional regulation, pattern recognition, and adaptive decision-making. When stress remains chronically elevated and HRV declines, the brain tends to shift toward threat detection and reactive processing instead.

In practical terms, this means the physiological state of the nervous system influences not only how overwhelmed we feel, but also how clearly we think, how creatively we problem-solve, and how effectively we navigate uncertainty.

In the context of leadership and business performance, restoring autonomic flexibility is therefore not simply a matter of stress reduction. It is part of maintaining the physiological conditions that allow insight, discernment, and strategic thinking to emerge.

Case Studies

When the system is in sympathetic overdrive, everything can feel urgent, compressed, and difficult to sort. Problems stack on top of each other. Decisions loop. The pressure to fix or resolve keeps the whole system activated.

In this state, change doesn't usually begin with a new strategy. It begins with seeing what is already there, without reacting to it in the same way. As that activation begins to settle, a pattern emerges. A thread begins to stand out from what once felt like separate problems.

In each of the cases that follow, that thread takes shape as a theme. Not something imposed, but something that emerges through the process itself through reflection, unwinding, and allowing what is there to be seen without immediately reacting to it. What once felt overwhelming or unworkable starts to reorganize around it.

The circumstances may not change right away, but the way they are held does. What felt like a closed loop begins to open. Something that couldn't be faced becomes something that can be worked with. From there, movement begins, less from force, more from a different relationship to what is unfolding.

Case Study #1: Rebuilding Capacity After Chronic Overwhelm

A high-performing professional sought coaching after experiencing a significant decline in health related to chronic stress and overwhelm in a demanding career. The accumulated strain eventually triggered an autoimmune condition, and her performance began to drop. She ultimately lost her job due to underperformance and entered coaching after trying an extensive range of conventional and alternative interventions without lasting improvement.

Her core belief at the start of our work was, "Success happens for other people, not for me." She had a pattern in which she would begin to improve, attempt to return to her previous workload, and immediately experience a relapse. Through coaching, she identified a critical insight: she could recover, but not if returning to the same career environment that had contributed to her illness.

We reframed her health challenge as an opportunity to design a career and lifestyle that matched her physiological needs and long-term goals. This involved clarifying the type of work that would support—not undermine—her health, identifying conditions necessary for sustainable performance, and redefining her criteria for success.

She transitioned into a new field that provided a supportive structure, improved lifestyle stability, and the income required to sustain her recovery. Her autoimmune symptoms went into remission, and she was able to maintain remission by using the lifestyle architecture she designed. As her capacity increased, she excelled in her new role and was later nominated for an award in her field—an outcome she initially believed was impossible.

Sustainable recovery and performance require modifying the systemic conditions driving dysregulation, not increasing individual effort. By aligning her work environment with her physiological capacity, the client stabilized her health, improved resilience, and reestablished long-term occupational viability.

Case Study #2: Processing What Isn't Yours to Carry

My client, Emmy, began her session feeling emotionally exhausted and physically taxed with strange digestive symptoms, nausea, and fatigue. At the same time, her business was expanding rapidly: her most recent class promotion had sold out in minutes, with a waitlist forming almost immediately. She'd launched new programs to complement her course schedule and serve a broader range of community needs, hired two staff members to support operations, and realized she now needed to double her income to sustain both her growing business and personal life.

The pressure of success was building. Beneath the excitement ran an undercurrent of guilt—for raising prices, for not having space for everyone, for the students who didn't get a spot. Even as her business flourished, she felt the weight of others' expectations pressing on her system.

Around the same time, her new home developed a sewage problem on a shared line with her neighbor, and the repair estimate was far higher than she expected. The situation required decisions about easements, legal agreements, and costs. More than the cost itself, it stirred a familiar emotional pattern: she found herself worrying more about how her neighbor might be impacted by her decision. She assumed installing a separate line would be an issue before she even knew the details.

As we explored, the poetic symmetry between her body, business, and home became clear. There was an overlapping energetic theme. As she experienced greater alignment and stability in these areas, an old pattern surfaced: the instinct to take responsibility for what wasn't hers to carry. Her digestion, her business stress, and her plumbing—she was processing other people's "waste."

Through the lens of the BizAttune process, we worked to further establish her business as its own energetic system—this time accessing the deeper remnants of attachment that kept her carrying its burdens in her body. We balanced the first chakra of her business (foundation, safety, and resources) with the third chakra (willpower, confidence, and action).

The first chakra had been expressing a "destructive" pattern: scarcity, instability, and the belief that when money comes in, it immediately goes out. It was now trying to evolve into a stronger foundation that allowed her to strategize beyond bare-minimum survival. The third chakra, by contrast, was strong and well-developed. Her ability to act decisively, follow through, and attract clients was undeniable. By linking the two, we allowed the stability of the first to receive the power of the third, transforming her business foundation into one capable of generating sustainable income, meeting expanding expenses, and growing with greater ease.

As the energy aligned, clarity emerged. The sewage issue mirrored a deeper truth: the need for clean boundaries—both physical and energetic—so her systems could flow freely. Separating the sewer line wasn't selfish; it was a declaration that she no longer needed to process anyone else's overflow.

By the end of our session, she recognized how this same pattern showed up in her relationships with clients. She anticipated their disappointment, absorbed their reactions, and felt guilty for her success. The shift crystallized in a single statement: "It's safe to get what I want."

My client noted afterward that looking at challenging situations through the lens of symbolism helps her stay centered. This was a powerful shift. Rather than being thrown off by disruption, she now sees each circumstance as information. It's an opportunity to notice what's mirroring back and ask, "How can I navigate this in a way that keeps me aligned with myself?" This way of relating transforms stress into stability and turns daily challenges into a practice of staying attuned.

Case study #3: When the Business Breathes on Its Own

Rachel arrived carrying a lot at once: a child's school transition stirring protective instincts, a wave of clients processing deep trauma, and the pressure to evolve a longtime service model into something more spacious and prosperous. She's a gifted empath and healer—so gifted that her business has been drawing on her personal capacity for emotional synthesis. In body terms, it showed up as the diaphragm doing double duty: she was "breathing for" her clients and her company.

In the session, we named the pattern: "I'm responsible for everyone." It echoed through family dynamics (old roles with a sibling and a father figure) and into business (long-term clients, loyalty, and the fear that growth might sever connection). Even the environment mirrored it in the form of background construction and household noise. Life was giving Rachel a test of whether her signal could stay steady amid interference.

We used the BizAttune process to separate her business as its own energetic system and relocated the work of emotional processing (the "diaphragm") into the business itself. That freed her body to return to her core frequency—what she calls her star. As soon as that shifted, the linkage rose from her diaphragm to her heart. Her heart and the heart of the business entrained, creating coherence instead of over-responsibility.

We then tuned two centers in the business consciousness: the first (or base) chakra (foundation, provisioning, and deserving) and the third chakra (willpower, execution, and magnetism).

Rather than operating from the survival energy of "I have to hold it all," we re-patterned the base to reflect a steady, rhythmic exchange: resources arrive in harmony with genuine need. This restored stability and allowed the business to become a true provider—supporting Rachel's family, creative life, and next-stage income growth without drawing on her personal reserves. We also anchored the frequency of deserving, so that her system could receive recognition and reward for the invisible emotional labor that had previously gone unseen.

The third chakra was already strong—she has no trouble showing up, creating, or leading. The shift was to root that strength down into the base so her drive could flow through stability rather than tension. By doing so, she began relating to business growth through constructive manifestation—seeing challenges, disruptions, and client needs as catalysts for alignment, not as burdens to carry. The business could now breathe, act, and expand without depending on her body's energy as its engine.

We also re-patterned family-of-origin energies. We repatterned Rachel's paternal ancestral genetics by disentangling a pattern of humiliation and "invisible labor" of being the one who always squeezes into the corner seat so everyone else can move freely.

Constructive manifestation became the organizing principle for growth. Obstacles serve alignment rather than stop it. Instead of "How will I do this?" we clarified the reward state: ease, provisions that support a creative family life, and prosperity with purpose. The frequency of deserving was integrated into this shift, allowing her to be seen and rewarded for work that had previously gone unnoticed.

Her somatic state calmed and settled. She told me, "My energy is coming back."

The business stopped pulling on her diaphragm and began breathing on its own.

From that shift came clarity. She could evolve the model by bringing long-term relationships forward into a renewed structure instead of carrying them somatically. What once had to be held together found its own order.

Case Study #4: Breaking Through the Upper Limit of Success

My client, Catherine, wrestled with following through on the key steps she knew would help her break through to new levels of success.

Things were going well—her annual revenue had finally hit mid–six figures after years of struggling to maintain consistency with her commissions. For the first time ever, she was cash-flow positive, debt-free, and still able to save. It was exhilarating and a huge relief.

But she worried it wouldn't last. "I keep waiting for the other shoe to drop," she told me. The dream of buying a house still felt out of reach, no matter how much she earned.

Then the panic set in.

She had never been here before. For so long, she had been the person who never had money, no matter how hard she worked. Now, the idea of being debt-free, saving, investing—even buying her dream home—felt overwhelming. Her nervous system didn't know how to make sense of it. Instead of relief, success triggered anxiety.

She was used to operating in a constant state of urgency, driven by catastrophic thinking and the fear of failure. Chaos, scarcity, and pressure had always pushed her forward. Without that familiar tension, she wasn't sure how to stay focused.

Without the intensity, how would she perform? For years, pressure had been the fuel for her performance.

She was facing one of the most common challenges that arise when someone breaks through to a new level of success:

"How do I become the version of myself who can sustain success once I achieve it?"

She knew exactly what she needed to do next, but follow-through felt impossible. Her nervous system was still wired for survival, and her old identity—"the one who never has enough"—was clashing with the new reality she had worked so hard to create.

This is when we shifted the strategy of our work together.

Rather than trying to push through the fear, we shifted the focus of our work toward helping her cultivate ease with success. We streamlined her schedule, created structures that supported predictability, and stabilized her revenue flow so her nervous system could settle. Most importantly, we worked at the identity level, uncovering the hidden habits and assumptions shaped by years of believing things wouldn't work out for her.

Once those unconscious patterns surfaced, she could finally see how her success had been colliding with an identity still organized around survival.

With clarity around her long-term vision, she stepped into the version of herself who was already successful, safe, resourced, and capable. As she let go of the belief that success required chaos, pressure, or urgency, she was finally able to take aligned action from a grounded, regulated place.

For her, the hardest part wasn't achieving success—it was learning to feel safe enough to sustain it. By uncovering the hidden habits rooted in scarcity, urgency, and survival, she was able to expand into a new identity—one defined by clarity, steadiness, ease, and self-trust.

Conclusion

For a long time, I felt like success was something that happened for other people, not me. There was a quiet expectation not to want too much, not to get my hopes up, because just as things were coming together, they could just as easily fall apart. That pattern took shape early, when my family began building what we believed would be our dream home, but just as it was coming together, it was never finished. Something in me learned to anticipate that same outcome in my own life—that even when things were working, they might not hold. Without realizing it, I carried forward the expectation that progress doesn't always lead to completion.

On the surface, I believed that if I worked hard enough and disciplined myself enough, I would eventually arrive at a place that felt like enough. What I did not understand then was that this was never about success. It was about trying to close a split.

Something deep within me was caught between longing to become that finished home and letting go of what was unfinished in order to become something else.

There was a split between what I knew and what I felt, between what I was told I should be working toward and what felt alive in my body, between practicality and purpose, between strategy and resonance. When I stayed in rooms that drained me because they were prestigious, I felt it in my body. When I sat in traffic commuting to the EPA job that looked responsible and adult but felt suffocating, my body knew. When I chose stability over vitality, when I tried to prove I was practical enough, serious enough, and employable enough, something inside me quietly contracted.

That contraction was not a weakness. It was intelligence.

Like many high performers, I inherited an unspoken equation: work harder, sacrifice more, earn your rest later. Scarcity was subtle but pervasive—scarcity of money, of opportunity, of security, of permission to want more. Overwork felt responsible. Ambition felt conditional. Desire felt risky.

I see now that much of my early striving was not ambition alone; it was inherited pressure. It was an internalized belief that I had to justify my existence through productivity.

Perhaps you recognize this pattern. Do you equate rest with laziness? Do you feel uneasy when things feel effortless? Do you measure your value by output? Do you quietly fear that if you slow down, everything will collapse?

Healing the inheritance of overwork and scarcity does not mean abandoning excellence. It means redefining the source of it.

My business eventually became the mirror that revealed the truth. Not because it failed and not because it succeeded, but because it reflected my coherence back to me with precision. When I was internally split, my business felt heavy. When I was overgiving, it drained me. When I was trying to prove my worth, it became performative. When I was aligned—when I honored my schedule in that job interview, when I chose dance despite practicality, when I followed the quiet yes into rooms that felt expansive—something reorganized.

It flowed.

That was when I began to understand something fundamental: intention organizes energy, but only when intention is aligned with essence. Not ego, not fear, not conditioning, but essence.

What I now call the BizAttune process was not something I invented. It was something I discovered. It is the organizing intelligence that emerges when your nervous system is regulated, your shadow is integrated, your boundaries are clear, and your desire is honest.

Business intuition and business energetics are not mystical add-ons. They are the practical development of this coherence. They are skills.

Peak performance, as I teach it, is not about pushing harder. It is about calibrating the system. It is about creating the biological and energetic conditions that naturally foster high-level decision-making, creativity, and resilience.

When coherence is present, decisions become cleaner. There is less internal debate and less self-betrayal. Red flags are harder to ignore. Timing feels intuitive rather than forced. You still work, you still stretch, you still take risks, but you are no longer performing worthiness. You are participating in alignment.

Think back to the moments in my life when everything shifted. Sleeping in the U-Haul in Hell's Kitchen and believing my dream had collapsed. Discovering Mabel Todd's *The Thinking Body* at exactly the moment I was doubting my path. Experiencing spontaneous qi rising through my body when I was not trying to make anything happen. Each of those moments was a recalibration point. Each one asked whether I would override myself again or listen.

Peak performance is not about closing the gap between where you are and where you want to be through force. It is about becoming nourished by the gap. The gap is not evidence of deficiency; it is tension that generates growth. In physiology, tension drives adaptation. In creativity, constraint generates innovation. In business, the edge between current capacity and future potential is where expansion happens.

What if the gap is not something to eliminate, but something to metabolize?

Traditional models of performance often treat uncertainty as a problem to eliminate. They promise that if you follow the right formula or replicate someone else's strategy, results will eventually appear. But growth rarely unfolds that way. Every meaningful endeavor contains ambiguity, risk, and incomplete information.

The real skill is not controlling uncertainty but navigating it. As you develop intuition, reflection, and coherence, you become capable of making decisions even when the outcome is not guaranteed. Over time, that capacity creates something far more valuable than a single successful result: it creates a person who can hold and sustain the life they are asking for.

What if instead of striving to close the gap, you learned to stand inside it?

Consider your current edge. Where do you feel called forward? Where do you feel intimidated by your own next level? Where are you minimizing your gifts to feel safe? Where are you overextending to feel secure?

Peak performance, in its truest form, is the capacity to remain steady at your edge, to expand without overwhelming your system, to grow without burning out, and to build without self-abandonment.

In a world where industries evolve faster than career ladders and artificial intelligence continues reshaping knowledge work, this capacity may become one of the most important leadership skills of our time. When information is unlimited but certainty is rare, the advantage shifts toward those who can remain steady while making decisions in uncertainty.

Personal peak performance is the alchemical process of transforming survival patterns into sustainable expansion. It is a manifestation in practice. It is not about forcing outcomes into existence; it is about becoming the version of yourself who can live easily inside the reality you are asking for.

Homeostasis is not simply a biological mechanism. It reflects how the body metabolizes experience, organizing its resources according to the patterns of living it has adapted to. When the body has adapted to chronic overwork and scarcity, the system organizes around stress. When safety is restored through alignment and integration, the system reorganizes around vitality. That is the deeper shift—not from failure to success, but from survival calibration to expansion calibration.

The vortex becomes your coach. It reflects where you are split, where you are aligned, and where coherence is present.

Through the work I do with clients, I help people learn how to access and work with this vortex consciously so their business and life begin organizing around coherence rather than pressure.

Through daily reflection and continued strengthening of business intuition, clarity increases and overwhelm decreases. Each setback becomes data. Each challenge becomes a refinement. Each contraction becomes information about where integration is still needed.

This approach redefines work as alchemy. Minimal force, maximum coherence. Constructive change instead of reactive effort. You develop an energy-intelligent business—one that you are in partnership with rather than fused to. Outcomes begin to support your becoming. The business no longer demands that you overextend to prove yourself. It reorganizes around the level of coherence you embody.

This is where business intuition becomes essential. Intuition, as we explored, is not guesswork. It is multiple parallel processing. It is the system synthesizing information beyond conscious tracking. It is the body recognizing patterns before the mind names them.

Intuition is the cultivation of a deeper form of pattern recognition that works alongside rational analysis rather than against it.

In my own life, I was often encouraged to dismiss inner knowing in favor of practicality. Yet when I followed only what appeared logical on paper, I remained stuck. The turning point came when I honored the quiet signals of intuition while still testing them against reality. Intuition opened the door to possibility; practical discernment determined how to move through it. When those two capacities work together, decisions become both grounded and expansive.

Distortion can arise in either direction. Listening to intuition without grounding it can lead to its own form of distortion. Some people bypass reality by ignoring data that contradicts what they hope to be true. That is magical thinking, not intuition.

The work of the vortex is to interrupt these habits. Surfacing unconscious assumptions and inherited pressures allows them to be integrated rather than unconsciously acted out. Intuition then becomes clearer, not because it replaces rational thinking, but because it is no longer clouded by fear, shame, or unexamined beliefs.

When your nervous system is chronically in overdrive, intuition becomes reactive and fear-based. When you recalibrate to steadiness, intuition becomes strategic and creative. Business energetics is the practice of clearing internal distortions—shame, scarcity, inherited pressure—so that your decisions reflect coherence rather than survival.

Many coaching models approach growth primarily as a problem-solving exercise: identify the obstacle, apply the right framework, and execute a strategy designed to produce a predictable result. Those tools can be helpful, but they assume that success can be engineered through formulas, protocols, or comparisons with what has worked for someone else.

The reality of entrepreneurship—and of life—is far more uncertain. The work described in this book shifts the focus from solving problems to strengthening decision-making under uncertainty. Rather than relying on external formulas, it develops the capacity to perceive patterns, interpret signals, and choose a direction that aligns with your values, vision, and deeper sense of purpose. The outcome is not dependence on a method but autonomy in decision-making.

From that place, something shifts. Energy reallocates. Attention sharpens. Boundaries strengthen. Creativity returns. Work begins to support you rather than consume you. You begin living with purpose instead of performing it.

You notice that success feels different in your body. It feels spacious instead of tight, energizing instead of draining, relational instead of isolating.

In many performance frameworks, success is defined almost entirely through measurable outcomes: revenue targets, growth metrics, or productivity benchmarks. Those indicators matter, but they tell only part of the story. When your decision-making becomes more coherent, success also begins to include qualitative dimensions—clarity, meaning, alignment, and the sense that what you are building reflects who you are becoming.

Over time, this shift changes the relationship you have with your business. Instead of working endlessly to sustain it, the business begins to support your evolution. Strategy becomes an expression of values rather than a reaction to pressure.

You do not have to dismantle your life to access coherence. You begin with awareness. Where does your body tighten when you consider your work? Where does it expand? Where are you performing instead of expressing? Where are you striving instead of standing in the present?

The vortex does not open because you force it open. It opens when you stop splitting yourself. It opens when you release the inheritance of overwork that tells you exhaustion equals virtue. It opens when you release the scarcity narrative that tells you safety requires self-suppression. It opens when you allow ambition to be fueled by vitality instead of fear.

If something in these pages resonated with you, it is likely because something in you recognizes the pattern. Perhaps you have built a career that looks successful but feels unsustainable. Perhaps you are capable and accomplished, yet quietly depleted. Perhaps you sense that your next level requires not more effort, but more alignment.

When you stop merging your identity with your output, your business no longer determines your worth. It reflects your coherence. From that place, your business becomes a partner. Your career becomes a conduit. Your goals become expressions of presence rather than proof of worth.

Peak performance, rather than something to strive for, emerges when the parts of you that once felt split begin working together again. Success stops feeling like something you must prove and starts feeling like something you can sustain.

This is the work I now guide others through—helping people transform pressure into coherence so their work, health, and ambition can expand together.

Within that process, business intuition is developed as a skill—learning to recognize, interpret, and act on the signals your system is already generating. The business itself becomes a separate energy system, something you can use as a focusing tool to recalibrate your internal baseline and strengthen your business intuition.

Goals and intentions begin to clarify and anchor in alignment, supported by accountability and the BizAttune vortex process, which reveals blind spots and brings into view what is actually happening as you move toward them. The vortex becomes a source of insight and momentum. Rather than forcing outcomes, there is a growing ability to read what is emerging, refine direction, and move with increasing precision. From there, daily practices take shape, creating traction that is both structured and responsive.

This is where the deeper work begins. As change unfolds, there is often a pull back toward what is familiar. Patterns shaped by overwork, scarcity, or instability can feel easier to return to than what is new. The work becomes one of unwinding those habituated patterns while gradually recalibrating the internal baseline so a different level of stability can hold.

Over time, something begins to reorganize. Goals evolve. Outcomes improve. Success itself is redefined—sometimes toward what is more aligned, sometimes toward what is more expansive than originally imagined. There is a growing capacity to recognize these shifts as they happen and to trust them.

It becomes less about applying a formula and more about becoming a coherent decision-maker—one who can navigate uncertainty, sustain growth, and create results that reflect both capacity and alignment.

By the end of this process, there is less reliance on rigid strategies, external formulas, or trial-and-error approaches. In their place is a capacity to work with the process itself—to interpret feedback, recalibrate in real time, and make decisions with clarity even when the path is not fully defined.

The foundations are in place to navigate both setbacks and successes in a way that is sustainable and regenerative over time. Goals begin to shift from something to chase into something to inhabit. The work becomes less about forcing outcomes and more about participating in what is unfolding.

The goal is not to follow a formula for success. It is to become the kind of decision-maker who can create success in many different forms. Success is not something you force into existence. It emerges when your decisions begin to reflect the coherence you have built within yourself.

You likely already sense your next step. If you choose to explore it, you do not have to do it alone. It may be small. It may be inconvenient. It may require courage. The question is not whether you are capable. You are. The question is whether you are willing to trust the part of you that already knows.

What is your next yes?

THANK YOU FOR READING MY BOOK!

Thank you so much for reading—it truly means the world to me! As my gift to you, scan the QR code below to schedule a free one-on-one call with me directly. No strings attached—just a genuine conversation about how I can best support your journey!

Scan the QR Code:

I appreciate your interest in my book and value your feedback, as it helps me improve future versions. I would appreciate it if you could leave your invaluable review on Amazon.com with your feedback. Thank you!

www.ingramcontent.com/pod-product-compliance
Lightning Source LLC
LaVergne TN
LVHW090520110826
845146LV00003B/929